Venture Capital Financing for Biotechnology

About the Authors

Dr. T. Satyanarayana Chary is Associate Professor, Department of Commerce, Telangana University, Nizamabad, Andhra Pradesh. He holds post-graduation degrees in Commerce (Gold Medalist) from Kakatiya University and Financial Management from Pondicherry University. He received the doctoral degree in Commerce and Business Management from Kakatiya University. His research work won the best paper award from Kakatiya University in the year 2004. He also secured consolation prize for his research paper on *Capital Account Convertibility—Makes the Elephant Dance* in the national research paper contest conducted by Indian Institute of Foreign Trade (IIFT) and 3rd best Ph.D. thesis award from Prestige Institute of Management & Research (PIMR), Indore. Very recently, he has secured the ISTD-ONGC best book award for his book on *Venture Capital—Concepts & Applications,* published by Macmillan India Limited.

Dr. Chary has published a number of articles and research papers in leading journals. His areas of specialization include Financial, Cost and Management Accounting, Financial Management, Security Analysis and Portfolio Management, Financial Services, Venture Capital and Financial Engineering.

Dr. R.K. Mishra, Senior Professor and Director, Institute of Public Enterprise, Hyderabad, India, a Ph.D. from the University of Rajasthan and a visiting fellow at London Business School, studied for International Teachers programme at SDA Bocconi, Milan. He taught at the University of Bradford, and was a visiting Professor at Maison Des Sciences De L' Hommes, Paris. He is a member of the UN Task Force on International Taskforce on Standards of Excellence in Public Administration and Education. His areas of interest include International Management, International Finance, Public-Private Partnership, Restructuring and Environmental Administration.

Venture Capital Financing for Biotechnology

T. Satyanarayana Chary
R.K. Mishra

CONCEPT PUBLISHING COMPANY, NEW DELHI-110 059

Cataloging in Publication Data—DK
Courtesy: D.K. Agencies (P) Ltd. <docinfo@dkagencies.com>

Satyanarayana Chary, T. (Thiruvarangam), 1972-
Venture capital financing for biotechnology / T. Satyanarayana Chary, R.K. Mishra.
p. cm.
With reference to India.
Includes bibliographical references (p.)
Includes index.
ISBN 13: 9788180695292
ISBN 10: 8180695298

1. Venture capital—India. 2. Biotechnology industries—India—Finance. I. Mishra, R. K. (Ram Kumar), 1948-, joint author. II. Title.

DDC 338.476 606 095 4 22

ISBN-13: 978-81-8069-529-2
ISBN-10: 81-8069-529-8

First Published 2008

Published and Printed by
Ashok Kumar Mittal
Concept Publishing Company
A/15-16, Commercial Block, Mohan Garden
New Delhi (INDIA)

Phones : 25351460, 25351794
Fax : 091-11-25357103
Email : publishing@conceptpub.com

Preface

Biotechnology is destined to be one of the prime determinants of our life styles and of the way we think and react to situations in the present century and the next. Like any such prime determinants such as space science, new sources of energy, new materials, computers, microelectronics, robotics, automation and artificial intelligence in history mankind can use biotechnology either wisely to maximize benefit to the largest number of people around the world.

Biotechnology industry has displayed many signs of evolving into a mature industry. Numbers of products, revenues, profits, market capitalisation are all up and show intrinsic value. The industry was trumpeted as the "greenshoots" of investment and stock market recovery in Europe and the US as more biotech-derived products came to the market. Half of the new drugs approved by the USA in 2003 were biologics. The industry ended the year 2003 building a diverse portfolio of protein therapeutics, many of which achieved blockbuster status. Though there was a decline in the total number of biotech companies both in the US and Europe, those surviving appears to have a firm financial base with a more realistic product portfolio.

India has already developed competence in selected areas and policy that provide the entrepreneurs an edge over other countries to set up viable and competitive biotech industry in certain areas. With its large resource pool of modern/molecular biologists, statisticians and software programmers, India seems well placed to garner most of the biotech market. Many Indian companies have introduced products of original research through technology transfer from R&D institutions of India in the field of vaccines, diagnostics and reagents. Some others have teamed up with foreign technologies with a view to introduce them into the Indian market within the framework of Indian laws. This situation is satisfactory to begin with, but there is tremendous scope to come up with innovative products that would be original and that would have cutting edge impact in the global context. Fresh investments of about US $ 1 billion in India could hold the potential of providing turnover of US $1.5 to 2 billion during the next 5 to 7 years, that could contribute import substitution, augmentation of local production and introduction of some new products for global marketing in the areas such as diagnostics, vaccines therapeutics, pharmacogenomics, bioinformatics, agriculture biotechnology, Industrial biotechnology, Inputs to the industry (hardware suppliers—instrumentation and chemicals), marine bio-prospecting and environment focused biotechnology. India is expected to emerge as a strong player in both manufacturing and consumption market of biotech products in the coming years.

Venture Capital (VC) is only the way of promoting and developing the biotechnologies for the betterment of the society as biotechnology is the cutting edge for venture capital in the present context. But before putting their hand, venture capitalists should understand well the Strength and Weakness as well as the benefits that they get from government in terms of incentives. Not only that, the venture capital funds need good human resource having expertise knowledge and specializing in specific biotechnologies, finance, marketing and technology forecasting. Finally, it can be asserted that the study helps as guide in understanding the linkage of venture capital with biotechnology and how to use venture capital to the new and budding entrepreneurs, entrepreneurs who are already in the field and how to perform the biotechnology finance by Venture Capital Companies/Funds.

Scarcity of VC continues to remain India's key challenge in developing the biotech industry. With the exception of few VCs, most VCs in the country are fairly new to this sector, do not quite understand the issues, are averse to risk and gestation periods involved, unlike in the US and Europe where a deep

VC industry has developed with many biotech sector focused funds.

The book points out the need for developing the awareness about VC in biotech industry and imminent strategies to be applied by venture capital funds in India to boost the unexploited areas of biotechnology in order to develop the new technologies for the benefit of the society. Moreover, it also points out that the problems and prospects of biotechnology projects in getting and utilizing the venture capital finance in India with special reference to selected venture capital funds and undertakings of those funds working in Andhra Pradesh.

To understand the existing Venture Capital System in Biotechnology Industry and find out the knowledge gap as well as problems in using Venture Capital for financing Biotechnology, we interacted with selected entrepreneurs of Biotechnology Industry and Venture Capital Funds. The conclusions drawn based on such interactions and feed back have been documented as part of the study.

We are grateful to our President Padmabushan Prof. Rama Rao, Shri Valluri Narayan, IAS (Retd.), President, IPE for his kind support and motivation in all our endeavours. We are thankful to our faculty colleagues for their continuous support, encouragement and guidance in the conduct of the study.

We are also thankful to Mr.E.V.Mahesh Kumar, and Ms T. Sreevani for their research support.

T. Satyanarayana Chary
R.K. Mishra

Contents

1
Introduction

Biotechnology could be defined as the application of organisms, biological processes to manufacturing and service industries (Coombs, 1986). Alternatively, biotechnology could be considered as commercial exploitation of living organisms or their components (Primrose, 1987). Yet another definition is provided by the Office of Technology Assessment of the USA, which defines biotechnology as any technique that uses living organisms, or substances from those organisms, to make or modify a product to improve plants or animals or to develop micro-organisms for specific uses (OTA, 1989). Karl Ereky, a Hungarian engineer, first coined the word biotechnology in 1919. At the time, the term referred to all lines of work involved in creating products from raw materials with the aid of living organisms. Today, the Biotechnology Industry Organization (BIO) defines biotechnology as "the use of cellular and molecular processes to solve problems or make products."

Biotechnology is a technology based on the use of tools such as vitro tissue and cell culture techniques, molecular methods and recombinant DNA technology that are used to modify the genetic make-up and generate new products, which give researchers a new capability of modifying crop plants to produce natural components more effectively and even to produce unexpected materials.

Biotechnology is often referred to as an 'enabling' technology, that is, a technology which triggers wider applications in a number of industries, including:

(1) Health—Pharmaceuticals diagnostics, gene therapy, biomedical products, medical devices and equipment.

(2) Agriculture—Plant and animal breeding, veterinary products and diagnostics.
(3) Environment and resources—Pollution control, land bio-remediation, water treatment, minerals extraction and processing, wastewater treatment, salinity control and pest management.
(4) Food and beverage processing—Starters, enzymes, fermentation, food ingredients fractionation.
(5) Industrial applications—Agriculture product processing (oils, fiber, etc.), bioprocess, and industrial enzymes.
(6) Energy production—Biomass.

Biotechnology has become the growing sector in international economy as we make transition form one millennium to another. It involves application of biological organisms, systems or processes to the manufacturing and service industries. The current trends in the sector show tremendous growth opportunities and it is being considered as a sunrise industry and is ranked at par with IT by experts. This is a field, which can revolutionize the growth prospects of a developing country. In the context of developing countries, agriculture has immense value. There are multiple uses of biotechnology techniques, and they have the potential of significantly influencing the economy of a country. They are expected to result in increased agricultural production; improved comparative advantage in production of some commodities new opportunities for the use of marginal lands and a reduced need for agrochemicals (World Bank, 1990). Biotechnological techniques can help to improve the tolerance of both crops and animals to specific stresses, pests, and pathogens and to increase the efficiency with which plants and livestock utilize limiting nutrients.

Information Technology *versus* Biotechnology

The biotechnology industry is similar to information technology industry populated by a large number of entrepreneurial high technology firms. On the other hand, comparison between success of Information Technology and Biotechnology expose complications in management of biotechnology. A Comparison of Biotech to Information technology based on various attributes is clearly analysed in Table 1.1.

Table 1.1.: Information Technology *versus* Biotechnology

Attributes	*Information Technology*	*Biotechnology*
Capital Investment	Low	High
Product Development Time	Less than 1 year	3-10 years
Product Development Cost	Low	High
Regulatory Control	Few	Many
Failure Risk	Low	High
Entry Barriers	Low	High
IPR costs and values	Low	High
Market size	Medium to Large	Small to Medium
VC understands	Good	Poor
Market Size of Service	>$ 100 billion (software)	<$ 10 billion (CROs)
Cross-licensing	High	Medium to high
Public acceptance	High	Low (sensitivities)

Source: Jone and Hine (2004).

Biotechnology Value Chain

Value is the difference between what customers are willing to pay and the cost of producing the value (Porter, 1990), the value chain in biotechnology is considered to be set of activities that are interconnected in an organization and together deliver value to customer, in the form of a product or service. The organizational value chain is the part of a larger stream of activities carried out by other entities, such as suppliers, distributors and customers. A detailed study by Jone and Hine (2004) identified eight definable elements that constitute the biotechnology value chain; they are:

1. basic research,
2. applied research,
3. development,

4. verification and validation,
5. prototype development,
6. clinical/field trials,
7. production/manufacturing, and
8. marketing.

These major elements of the value chain have sub-activity or sub-task to cater for unique differences between biotechnology products and companies. The value chain analysis of biotechnology is shown in Figure 1.1.

Figure 1.1: The Value Chain of the Biotechnology

1. Basic Research 2. Applied Research	1. Development 2. Verification 3. Prototype development 4. Clinical/field trials	1. Production/ manufacturing 2. Marketing.

Discovery		**Development**			**Commercialisation**	
Idea generation	Application	Optimization	Quality control	Phase I	Production	Price
Idea evaluation	Proof of principle	Testing	Pre-clinical testing	Phase II	Scale-Up	Promotion
Feasibility	IP generation		Regulatory	Phase III	Standardization	Distribution
Concepts				Registration	Validation	Sale & service

Source: Jone and Hine (2004).

The above value chain is basically applicable to manufacturing of health care products, industrial biotechnology and food and beverage processing. In Agriculture, predominant biotechnology application is production of genetically engineered seeds or genetically modified (GM) seeds. Steps in R&D to seed marketing would take 8-10 years along the value chain after clearances from regulatory prospective and several millions of dollars. However, based on the above analysis it can be identifiable that managerial skills and decisions in terms of planning and execution of biotechnology projects are involved at a number of stages of the value chain towards commercialization of biotechnology. Hence, the five key stages of management that involves in the biotechnology projects are: Research and Development, Regulation, Intellectual property, financial management and managing transition.

Impact of Biotechnology on Economy

It is as off-putting a task today to decide how biotechnology will affect future economic activity as it might have been for economists in the 18th, 19th and 20th centuries to forecast how the steam engine, electricity and the microchip would influence and eventually transform the world economy. With the assistance of mind-boggling inventions, humankind's bucolic existence has morphed into a world that our agrarian ancestors would scarcely recognize. Biotechnology may change our world as much. Even though the bioscience industry has been around for 25 years and the gargantuan task of mapping the human genome is complete, it's still not clear to what extent life science technology will affect our economy. Some observers have already labeled this the "Biological Century," betting that advances in the life sciences will yield changes more momentous than those of electricity and computers. Such predictions may be over inflated, but biotechnology has the potential to greatly affect the economy.

Two types of economic effects are already appearing in the nascent industry. By analogy, they resemble the direct splash of a stone tossed into a pond and the indirect rippling that follows. Direct impacts from biotechnology include such obvious pluses as research and development (R&D) spending, sophisticated jobs and tax revenues. Biotech companies have already sprouted up in many parts of the country. Less visible are the indirect effects, which include improvements in quality of life and living standards stemming from faster labor productivity growth, better health products and services, and a cleaner environment.

In May 2000, BIO commissioned Ernst and Young to determine the aggregate impact of biotechnology firms on the

U.S. economy. The study looked at information from firms whose primary business operations fell under five Standard Industrial Classification codes. While some components of biotech activity are not included in this definition, the report gives an idea of the direct impact the bioscience is having on the economy. The study reveals impressive growth for the industry. The life science industry more than doubled revenue from $8 billion in 1993 to $20.2 billion in 1999. R&D spending was $11 billion in 1999, not counting monies spent by colleges, universities and nonprofits. Total tax collections reached nearly $10 billion. Federal taxes accounted for $6.8 billion of the total and state and local taxes for the remainder.

Completion of the human genome and promises of new medicines sent biotech share prices skyward in 1999 and 2000. Since then, sparse profits and the realization that investment returns to biotechnology are going to take some time has kept overall stock prices subdued. Profitability in the four largest biotech firms has instilled recent confidence in the sector, but the majority of firms have yet to show a profit. Overall health care and prescription drug expenditures have increased steadily in recent years. For example, health care expenditures as a percentage of GDP have grown from 8.8 per cent in 1980 to 13 per cent in 2000. Prescription drug expenditures have been climbing steadily since 1994. Recognizing the growth potential in the industry, 41 states, including Texas, New Mexico and Louisiana, are currently pursuing economic initiatives to foster growth in their emerging biotechnology sectors.

Still a relative newcomer to the economy, biotechnology is already having a positive indirect influence on economic activity. Ernst and Young estimates that biotechnology has an employment multiplier of 2.9. In other words, each job created in biotech generates an additional 2.9 jobs, resulting from biotech firms' purchases and consumer spending of biotech employees. With the multiplier effect, biotech's total impact on employment comes in at more than 4,37,000 jobs.

Ernst and Young gives biotech a 2.3 revenue multiplier, increasing the total impact on revenues from biotechnology to $46.5 billion. The personal income multiplier is estimated to be 2, which results in a $28.8 billion total impact on personal income from the industry. Biotechnology's contributions to medicine and health care are growing rapidly, promising to increase human longevity and healthiness. To the extent that biotechnology results in new treatments for old ailments, people will become more productive over their lifetimes.

In addition, improved strains in agricultural crops have helped increase yields for many years. Research and development of more-productive and disease-resistant crops have enabled output per farmer to increase steadily. Improvements in quality of life will continue as scientists further harness biological processes to clean up hazardous waste and contaminated areas. Environmental remediation is growing fast as a result of increased public demand for a cleaner, safer and more natural living space. However the impact of biotechnology on economy, society and the environment is very high presently and in coming future, also.

Need for the Study

We are in the era of indispensable liberalization, inevitable privatization and invincible globalization, where change is playing a dominant and pervasive role. It is due to such environment, coping with change through new and innovative technologies have become the order of the day. In this regard, after leading the IT bandwagon, India has shifted its focus to Biotechnology. The developments in the area of biotechnology are particularly of great interest. This frontier technology becomes important in a developing country like India where agriculture, with stagnating productivity and crops confronting many biotic and a biotic stress, aims for higher growth. The industrial sector is expecting a change in production profile with new molecules and new enzymes.

India spends about 1 per cent of the GDP on science and technology research. As in other areas of technology, biotechnology research is mostly funded by public money. India possesses adequate human resources to carry out biotechnology research, but it lacks well-defined policy and programme. There are very few private sector companies and public sector activities dedicated to biotechnology. The cooperation between educational institutes, research and development organizations, and industry is low, only limited venture capital finance is available and India also does not have patent protection and environmental laws. So, it is the need of the hour of financing biotechnology through venture capital in India to make her to leap into the sea of development. So an attempt is made in the study entitled Development and Promotion of Biotechnology through Venture Capital with a greater expectation of insights about the promotion and financing of biotechnology by venture capital funds in India and the ability of the biotech industry in exploiting the new technologies with the help of venture finance as a new source of capital. It also covers the imminent strategies to be applied by venture capital funds in India to boost the unexploited areas of biotechnology in order to develop the new technologies for the benefit of the society. Moreover, it is also expected that this study would contribute in identifying the problems and prospects of biotechnology projects in getting and utilizing the venture capital financing in India.

Objectives of the Study

The main objective of the study is to analyse the role of venture capital in developing and promoting the new and groundbreaking technology i.e. Biotechnology, companies in Andhra Pradesh. Though the perspectives of selected biotech ventures financed by different venture capital funds, hence, the specific objectives are:

(1) To study the importance of development and promotion of biotechnology in the new economic era and examine the linkage between venture capital and biotechnology.
(2) To study the policies of selected venture capital funds/ companies in promoting and developing the biotechnological companies.
(3) To find out the problems of bio-tech units financed by venture capital funds/companies.

(4) To evaluate the role of venture capital funds/firms in promoting the first generation biotech scientists/ entrepreneurs through the perspectives of selected units in Andhra Pradesh.

(5) To find out the needs and the knowledge gap of biotech units towards venture capital.

Scope and Limitations of the Study

The study is very comprehensive in nature. It covers the concept of venture capital and its application and role in developing biotechnologies. The study was carried out based on five venture capital undertakings (biotech firms) financed by different venture capital funds, so the problems of sample units may not represent all the types of biotech undertakings financed under venture capital scheme. Validity of the inferences drawn is subject to the time as point of responses given by the respondents.

Methodology

Sample

As the study's main focus is on the role of venture capital in Developing and Promotion of Biotech units in Andhra Pradesh, five biotech undertakings/investee firms financed by different venture capital funds were taken as sample through list sampling method. Out of 5 companies selected, two were in pipeline of getting venture capital and the rest three were financed by A.P.I.D.C.-Venture Capital Limited and IDBI Venture Capital Fund. Profile of the sample companies is explained well in the respective chapter.

Data Sources and Analysis

The study on Development and Promotion of Biotechnology through Venture Capital is a survey method of study. Needed data was collected from both primary and secondary sources. Primary data was collected through field survey by administering a well-prepared questionnaire to selected biotech undertakings financed by venture capital funds/companies in Andhra Pradesh. And the secondary data was collected through literature concerned i.e. articles, working papers, research on the topic and other sources related.

Data thus collected was processed, analyzed and interpretated to draw the valid inferences. For analyzing the data and proving the realities of the research out comes ratio analysis, percentages, pie-diagrams/charts etc., were employed.

Time Span of the Study

The time span of the study was one-a-year.

Design of the Study

The study on Development and Promotion of Biotechnology through venture capital is divided into eight chapters, which as follows:

Chapter 1 Introduction: It deals with the concept and execution of the study i.e. Research Methodology.

Chapter 2 Biotech Industry: Global and Indian Scenario: An attempt has been made in this chapter to analyze the emergence of biotechnology, global trends of biotechnology and Indian biotechnology industrial scenario.

Chapter 3 Policy Environment of Biotechnology Industry in India: It deals with government policy towards biotech industry and the changes that have been taken place in recent past in the policy itself.

Chapter 4 Government Funding of Biotechnology: This chapter discusses on the role of government in biotechnology finance through institutional set-up and budgetary allocations in five years plan.

Chapter 5 Venture Capital Financing of Biotechnology: This chapter is devoted to analyze the role of venture capital in promotion and development of biotechnology in a broader perspective.

Chapter 6 Profiles of Major Venture Capital Funds: It discusses about the brief history selected major venture capital funds and the undertakings financed by APIDC-Venture Capital Limited and IDBI Venture Capital Fund and others.

Chapter 7 Perceptional Analysis of the Selected Biotech Companies: This chapter is a modest attempt to analyze the perception of selected venture capital undertakings over various issues of venture capital scheme provided by companies concerned. Also it covers the analysis over the knowledge gap between the entrepreneurs and venture capital funds.

Chapter 8 Towards a New framework of Financing Biotechnology: This chapter presents summary of findings in terms of conclusions and suggestions.

Chapter 9 Case Study of M/s. Jayaprada Clonetech Pvt. Ltd.

2

Biotech Industry: *Global and Indian Scenario*

The Biotechnology industry is playing a dominant role in the present techno-economic era, in fact it is the industry outpacing Software industry over the world. However this field is dominated by the private industry in developed countries with the MNC's playing a leading role. Undoubtedly, the entire globe is at the dawn of another revolution fuelled by biotechnology. In 2003 global biotech industry includes more than 4300 companies (613 of these are publicly traded) throughout the USA, Canada, Europe, Australia/New Zealand, and Asia applying revolutionary discoveries in science to tackle the planet's toughest health care, agricultural, industrial and environmental challenges (Ernst and Young, 2003).

Biotechnology is an emerging sector in Asia/Pacific experiencing notable expansion in India, Australia, China and Singapore. Global market for biotechnology applications will reach US$50 billion annually by 2005 where the strongest growth is projected for agri-food sector. Global value for genetically modified crops grew from US$75 million in 1995 to US$1.64 billion in 1998 and projected at 46 billion by 2005 and to 20 billion by 2010 (Clive James 2003). It is also estimated that by 2005 European biotech market could double from current valuations to more than $100 billion.

Many studies proved that the biotechnology has greater promise in developing countries like South Asian countries because of their high reliance on agriculture (for income and employment of the large population) coupled with low crop yield, which is detrimental for these countries as latter erode the level playing field for these countries in agricultural trade under liberalized trade policy. In this regard some of the developing countries such as Mexico, Argentina, China and Chile have already made considerable economic advances by integrating biotechnology into their agricultural programmes. Others such as Cuba, Egypt and South Africa are also following close behind and clearly see towards biotechnology as a means of advancing their economies. India is also striving hard to solve so many vexing problems with which it is combating through biotechnology such as providing nutritional security to its ever-burgeoning population, large chunk of who are already malnourished, population presser on land because of intensive land use and widespread biomass shortage, cultivated soils are being depleted of essential nutrients and organic matter, increasing strain of Fisheries, livestock and forestry etc.

Some of the achievements in biotechnology include tissue culture regeneration, stress biology, and maker-assisted breeding, as well as new types of bit fertilizer and biopesticide formulations. Research to develop genetically improved (transgenic) plants for brassicas, mung bean, cotton and potato is well advanced. Programs adapted to local needs and priorities are under way in countries like Philippines, Thailand, Brazil, Costa Rica, Mexico, Egypt, Iran, Jordan, Kenya, South Africa, and Zimbabwe. Of particular interest for Africa, the research results are thriving well on the transgenic sweet potato resistant to feathery mottle virus in Kenya and on South African transgenic sweet potatoes that contain up to five times the normal protein levels.

In many countries, tissue culture has produced and provided planting material to the farmers that increased crops' yields manifold. In addition, market assisted selection and DNA fingerprinting allows a faster and more targeted development of improved genotypes for important agricultural species. Moreover, these technologies make available new research methods, which can assist in the conservation and characterization of biodiversity. These new techniques will enable scientists to recognize and target quantitative trait loci and increase the efficiency of breeding for some traditionally intractable agronomic problems such as drought resistance and improved root systems.

Biotechnology Industry: Indian Scenario

The Indian biotechnology industry has its roots in fermentation technology, enzyme production, genetic engineering and tissue culture. The eighties was the capability-building phase during which a number of institutions were established, such as Centre for Cellular and Molecular Biology (CCMB) at Hyderabad, National Institute of Immunology (NII) etc. Similarly two entrepreneurial came up and it was supported by venture capital that signaled the start of biotech industry growth in India. The second phase of the evolution of biotechnology in India was the strengthening of the institutions, especially the research institutions which became a player in contract research. Shantha Biotech came up with India's first recombinant product, Hepatitis *B* Vaccine. Monsanto started Bt Cotton trials. Many global firms started R&D centres in India. The third phase was essentially the evolution of the entrepreneurial phase. The chronology of biotechnology industry in India from 1978 to 2005 is given in Table 2.1.

The salient features of Indian Biotechnology industry are: (1) Investment in R&D has been low in India in comparison with global firms as India lags behind in knowledge creation with respect to biotechnology industry, (2) As it has an advantage in bioinformatics with leading IT firms in India getting active in bioinformatics, (3) India lags behind in infrastructure compared to the other developing countries such as Brazil, Taiwan, China, Israel etc.,(4) Though many universities are working on biotechnology, they have not contributed much to the growth of biotech industry because of weak industrial interface and product development capabilities , and (5) Small number of entrepreneurial firms coming up in biotechnology. Hence, with such features India entered the fast changing biotechnology industry even though conventional biotechnology has been practiced in India for several decades. It is estimated that there are more than

Table 2.1: Evolution of Indian Biotechnology Industry

Year	Event
1978	Country's first biotech company BIOCON for industrial enzymes.
1981	Center for Cellular and Molecular Biology (CCMB) for DNA and r-DNA based research.
1984	Institute for Microbial Technology, (IMTECH) for R&D in microbial bio-processing.
1986	Department of Biotechnology (DBT), set up by Government of India for promoting modern biology and biotechnology at academic and industry levels.
1987	National Institute of Immunology (NII) setup by DBT for immunology research.
1989	Bangalore Genei starts operations to produce restriction enzymes and other tools for DNA based R&D.
1991	Four National Center for Biological Sciences (NCBS) to pursue R&D molecular biology.
1994	Syngene International, country's first CRC (promoted by Biocon) to offer R&D services in drug discovery based modern biology.
1997	Center for Biochemical Technology (CBT) to focus on Bioinformatics and Genomics.
1997	Shantha Biotech launches India's first recombinant product, Hep B vaccine.
1998	Monsanto research establishes an R&D center at IISc for plant genomics.
1998	DBT approves Mahyco-Monsanto to conduct Bt cotton trials.
2000	Four states Andhra Pradesh, Karnataka, Maharashtra and Tamil Nadu announce Biotech initiatives.
2000	Country's first Bioinformatics company Strand Genomics formed by four IISc professors.
2000	GENOMED country's first JV between Institute (CBT) and Industry (Nicholas Piramal) to pursue pharmaco-genomics.
2001	NCBS scientist sets up Avesthagen a plant genomics company.
2001	GEAC approves Wockhardt's EPO.
2001	NIH approves NCBS and Reliance Life Sciences as 2 out of 10 labs worldwide, for stem cell lines.
2001	Drug Authority implements GCP guidelines for clinical trials.
2001	Millennium biotech policy, the first state level Biotech policy, announced by Government of Karnataka.
2002	Institute of Bioinformatics and Applied Biotechnology a jointly funded initiative between Government of Karnataka and ICICI commences academic program.
2002	GEAC approves Bt cotton for commercial planting.
2002	GEAC approves Shantha Biotech's Interferon Alpha 2b.
2002	WHO Approves Shantha Biotech's hepatitis B vaccine.

Source: www.biotech-india.com

800 companies in India spanning various sectors of biotechnology as shown in Table 2.2. A few companies have launched their products, based on tissue culture. One such big plant was set up in Cochin. Several pharmaceutical firms are marketing immuno-diagnostic kits for the early detection of pregnancy and diseases like amoebiasis, hepatitis and typhoid. Recently, an indigenously developed kit for early detection of pregnancy was launched. Many other diagnostics kits are likely to touch the market soon. The Government of India has approved a number of new industrial licenses/foreign collaborations in the area of agriculture, environmental and food biotechnology, and yet many more are under active consideration.

Table 2.2: Indian Biotechnology Industry

Parameter	*Status*
Biotechnology market	$4 billion
Employment	20000 people
India's share in global biotechnology market	2%
Consumption of biotechnology products in India by 2005	Rs.145870 million (IUSD = 48 INR)
Firms operating in the biotechnology sector	800
Firms working in modern biotechnology	Approximately 40

Source: IBID data base.

Segmentation of the Industry

Indian Biotech industry can be divided broadly into different segments as Medical Biotechnology, Agri Biotech, Services segment and others as shown in Figure 2.1.

It is estimated that vaccines, contract research, agriculture and human health sectors comprise as much as two thirds of the total market. It is further estimated that health care products would dominate the Indian biotech market, roughly 40 per cent the total market by the year 2010 followed by agriculture about 30 per cent. It is also estimated that contract research and bioinformatics would pick up and account for as much as 25 per cent of the biotech market. An estimation by CII shows that the Agri-Biotech would see growth rates of as much as 60 per cent, Diagnostic and Therapeutics about 25 per cent and Vaccines about 15 per cent. These figures clearly indicate the prospects of the Biotech industry in India. Hence, the exact sectoral break up of biotech market can be seen from the Figure.

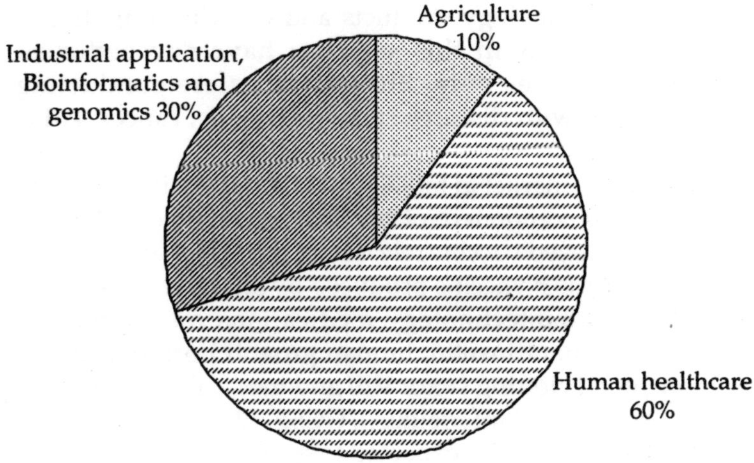

Fig 2.1: Segmentation of Indian Biotechnology Industry

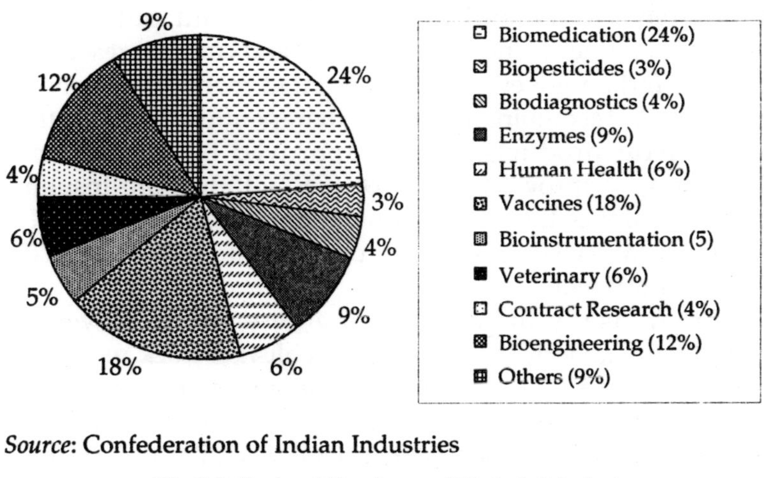

Source: Confederation of Indian Industries

Fig 2.2: Sectoral Break up of Biotech Market

Human Healthcare Segment

This is the largest segment in the industry and it accounts for $2.4 billion. The majority of firms in this segment concentrate on high volume-low value products like vaccines and biological enzymes. These firms have yet to achieve capability to create innovative biotechnology products and carrying out clinical trials. So far, firms in this segment have succeeded in introducing vaccines only. But few firms are conducting research to deal with diseases such as diabetic, cancer, AIDS etc.

The vaccine market in India, valued at approximately $150 million, is a key component of the healthcare sector. The first biotechnology-based vaccine released in the Indian market was an rDNA hepatitis B vaccine produced by Shantha Biotechnics Pvt. Ltd. Other biotechnology medications on the market include recombinant insulin, human growth hormone, alpha interferon, blood clotting factor VIII and medical proteins such as relaxin, rennin and interleukins, GCSF, EPO and Interferon Alpha 2b. The year 2003 is expected to see the launch of human insulin, streptokinase, other vaccines and diagnostics. The diagnostics market is valued at an estimated $75 million and is dominated by demand for monoclonal and polyclonal antibodies, tissue typing, clinical assays and contract research.

The Indian government has granted marketing licenses for about 25 recombinant protein therapeutics. Some of the recombinant products already approved by the Genetic Engineering Approval Committee (GEAC), they are Insulin, Interferon alpha, Interferon gamma, Interleukin-2, Gm-CSF, G-CSF, Hepatitis B vaccine, Erythropoietin, Streptokinase, EGF and Chymotrypsin.

Traditionally India has been a very strong player in conventional generic drugs due to established track record of process engineering skills and capability to set up comparable manufacturing units at a fraction of the capital cost utilised overseas. Companies such as Shantha biotechnics that started with just one product are now effectively using this experience to launch other products like plasminogen activators, interferons, sophisticated vaccines etc. After the liberalization of the Indian Economy many multinationals like Monsanto, Pfizer, Unilever, Dupont, Bayer, have set up their businesses in India. Eli Lilly—Ranbaxy 50:50 joint venture in India has been marketing a range of biotech products such as Humalog and Huminsulin for diabetes. Hoechst Roussel Vet has developed a cow abortion IBH vaccine in India. Chiron-Boehringer is setting up a vaccine venture in India. The major players of healthcare segment and their product profiles are given in Table 2.3.

Table 2.3: Major Players In The Healthcare Segment

Company Name	*Technology*	*Products*	*International patents*
Bharat Biotech	Genetic Engineering	Hepatitis B Vaccine Streptokinase Human Insulin	1
Biological Evans		Vaccines For Polio, Tetanus, Hepatitis	—
Bharat Immunological		Polio Vaccine	—
Shantha Biotechnics	Genetic Engineering	Hepatitis B Vaccine	1
Torrent Scietech		Hepatitis B Vaccine Penicillin-G	—

Source: IBID data base and respective company profiles.

Agri Biotech Segment

India is the world's largest producer of fruits and vegetables that accounts only for 1 per cent of total world exports as Indian agriculture is often inefficient and plagued by pests. The potential of agricultural biotechnology to feed the people of India and increase export markets for Indian products is significant. Transgenics of rice, brassica, moonbean, pigeonpea, cotton, tomato and some vegetables like cabbage, cauliflower etc. will complete field assessment and some of them would be ready for large scale production by 2005. High protein wheat with high lysine content will be introduced in the farmer's field by 2003-2005. India is the world's third-largest cotton producer in terms of area, but with yields of approximately 300 kg. per hectare, the country produces far below the global average of 650 kg. per hectare. Bt Cotton is an important innovation that can benefit India.

The agriculture market is presently estimated as $0.4 billion. US-based Hicks Muse's proposal to take up 75 per cent equity in India Seed Holding through its Mauritius subsidiary has been cleared by the government. The company will invest US$ 35 million for production and marketing of hybrid and improved variety of seeds. The Indian partner in this venture is Mahindra Hybrid Seeds, Bayer New Delhi based Pro-Agro group companies. But to date, only a small number of companies and research institutions have been allowed to conduct field trials on GM crops viz., rice, maize, cotton, tomatoes and cauliflower. The major firms active in this segment are given in Table 2.4.

Table 2.4: Major players in the Agribiotech sector

Company Name	*Product segment*
Khoddy Biotech and A.V. Thomas Biotechnology	Tissue Culture
Mahyco	Plant Breeding, Pathology
Spic	Hybrid seeds
Sun Agro Industries	Seed Multiplication

Source: IBID data base and respective company profiles.

With increase in population and concern about the quality of food, the bioagriculture has gained focus in the recent past in India. The farmers in India are looking at the GM seeds, biofertilizers, biopesticides from which they can expect more return on their investments. The farmers are now getting a premium for the organic produce. With which now they are able to export their produce at much higher price. The agribiotech market in 2002-03 was Rs. 110 crore.

The challenge of producing more food grains to feed the ever increasing population of India that has already crossed one billion mark with less resources has bought companies like

Mahyco, Monsanto, Syngenta, ProAgro, Advanta to invest in GM crops. It was in 2002 a joint venture between Mahyco and Monsanto called Mahyco- Monsanto Biotech Ltd. got the green signal from the Government of India for the commercial production and sale of Bt cotton (Bollgard) in six southern states of India. It was able to sell most of its Bt cottonseeds produced by Mahyco. Looking at the demand for Bt cottonseeds, Gujarat-based Navbharat Seeds is believed to have sold Bt cotton unofficially in the parts of Gujarat before the launch of Bollgard.

Meanwhile, recently GEAC has rejected Monsanto's proposal for commercial production of Bt cotton in north India. This has pushed it to enter into a tie up with other local companies to produce different varieties of Bt cotton that will suit the conditions in north India. More companies like Mahendra and Paras of the Emergent group, Nath Seeds, Ankur Seeds, Ajeet Seeds, Raasi Seeds, Krishi Dhan, JK Agrigenetics and Nuziveedu Seeds are working on releasing Bt cotton. These are expected to be ready for release in 2006. Further work is being done on GM maize/corn, mustard, soyabean and rapeseed. Companies are already doing research and conducting field trails on these crops.

A lot of awareness campaigns have to be conducted to reach out to the farmers to brief them about the benefits of using seeds that are resistant to pests, diseases, herbicides, and crops which are tolerant to drought, cold, salinity and other harsh environments. Amid mixed response to the Bt cotton (Bollgard), the government has to monitor the potential of the GM crop before giving a final verdict. This will bring in confidence among the farmers as well as the industry people.

Biofertilizers/Biopesticides

In addition to GM seeds, the farmers are also looking at biofertilizers, biopesticides to get more benefits. Excel Industries, Ajay Biotech, EID Parry and many other companies are producing biopesticides/biofertilizers. Now the farmers are using formulations based on Bt, viruses like NPV, and GV, as well as neem-based pesticides. To meet the increasing demand, the industry has to scale up investments in biofertilizers and biopesticides. Conservative estimate shows that the 10 per cent saving through the use of biofertilizers will result in an annual saving of 1.094 million tons of nitrogenous fertilizers costing around Rs. 550 crore. Delhi-based Biotech International is one of the largest producers of biopesticides in the country.

Biofuel

Looking at the opportunity in biofuel sector, the central government has taken an initiative to promote this sector in a big way. The total consumption of ethanol-blended petrol is expected to be 4.6 million tons per year. This sector not only helps sugarcane farmers, as cane is used as raw material for production of ethanol, but also helps in building up the oil security apart from benefiting the environment. It can save foreign exchange to the tune of Rs. 80,000 crore, as India imports about 70 per cent of its requirement of crude oil. Praj Industries and Alfa Laval India have already commissioned plants to produce ethanol which will be operated on Molecular Sieve Technology. Few more plants are in pipeline.

Industrial Biotech Segment

This segment is expected to show significant growth commensurate with the growth of the Biotech sector. Products include enzymes, peptides, herbal extracts etc. Majority of these firms are export oriented and are mainly concentrating on process innovation to be competitive. Major players in this segment are given in Table 2.5.

Table 2.5: Major players in the industrial segment

Company Name	*Product Segment*
Ajay Biotech	Microbiology
Biocon India	Micro Array
Indfrag Biosciences	Botanical Extracts
RPG Life Sciences	Enzymes

Source: IBID data base and respective company profiles.

In recent years, the importance of enzymes in human biology and the potential for improved health through supplementation have contributed to greater renown for enzyme sector, an once obscure category. The bulk of the enzyme-supplement category consists of digestive enzymes. These are used in many industries like healthcare, starch processing, breweries and distilleries, industrial alcohol, textile processing, garment and denim washing, detergent and cleaning aids, leather processing, baking and flour milling, food processing, animal and fish feeds, natural extracts and waste treatment.

Enzymes have potential use in many ways in these sectors. In the textile sector, enzymes are used for desizing of fabric/ yarn, biopolishing, silk degumming and wool finishing applications. In the paper industry, it improves bleachability of all kinds of pulp. In the leather industry, enzymes help in rapid scud loosening, wetting and degreasing, removal of adhering fatty tissues from the skin and facilitates an optimum bating action. Enzymes also help in the treatment of collagen to dissolve it into gelatin solution. Its usage reduces viscosity of the gelatin or collagen solution and bloom. Apart from these, many more applications have attracted entrepreneurs to look at this sector as a lucrative one.

At present we find many companies in India that are manufacturing industrial enzymes. These include Biocon, Advanced Biochemicals, Maps India, Fermenta Biotech, Bharat Biotech, Excel Industries, Maple Biotech, Genetix Biotech Asia, Artemis Biotech, Proalgen, Sangitha Biochemicals, Krebs and others. Apart from being marketed in India, enzymes are exported to other Asian and European countries.

The bioindustrial sector was estimated to be Rs. 235 crore. For this segment analysis, enzymes, organic amino acids and yeast products were taken into consideration. Enzymes was the single largest market with sales close to Rs. 127 crore in revenues and accounted for 55 per cent of the market share. Organic amino acids accounted for 34 per cent of the market share.

Biocon has the distinction of being one of the first enzyme companies globally to receive ISO 9001 accreditation in 1993. To enhance its activities in manufacturing enzymes Biocon has tied up with one of the world's largest enzyme conglomerates-Genencor International and Quest International, an ICI subsidiary for select food enzymes. Its forte has been in creating niche markets through innovative enzymes and enzyme applications.

The product range and services are growing rapidly as the use of enzymes has gained wide spread acceptance. The companies are also looking at producing different types of industrial enzymes, using all the natural methods of production, from plants and vegetable origin, fermentation—both with solid state and submerge culture techniques. Companies are also spending on the R&D efforts directed not only towards development of new innovative products but also towards making them available at economical price to customers.

Hence, Industrial biotech is fairly wide ranging. It includes industrial enzymes; diagnostic and research enzymes, peptides etc; biotransformation for production of specialty chemicals, drug intermediates etc. However, as industrial biotech activity is relatively free from regulatory complexities of biopharma, transgenic plant development etc. is likely to grow at a relatively faster pace compared to other areas of biotech.

Services Segment

Biotechnology services are a growing segment having many new entrants. Normally a biotech based therapeutic product costs $250 million and takes 10-15 years to reach the global market. In India, the operational cost is estimated as one seventh of that in global market. This has given rise to contract research as an opportunity for firms specialising in drug discovery services. Contract Research services are largely focused on molecular biology, bioinformatics, genomics and stem cell research, cDNA library preparation, genetic research related to medical diagnosis, new crop varieties and early stage drug development. Clinical research and trials are expected to grow sharply in the next 5 years. This will in turn prompt many MNCs to start their operations in India. More bioinformatics firms are also entering into the market as India has strong capability in software development.

Bioinformatics is one of the major growth opportunities, it has proved indispensable for drug development and its fortunes are directly linked to the fortunes of the pharma industry. It is a useful tool to produce new crop varieties where opportunity lies. In 2000, Oscar Gruss, a market research company in the US had estimated the global Bioinformatics industry to be $2 billion by 2005. India has tremendous opportunities in bioinformatic sector for data mining, gene annotation, and the development of software interfaces. These require enormous computing power for which India has established its supremacy. In India, by the end of 2000, six bioinformatics companies had come up. Spectramind eServices of Delhi began with 20 PhD's to analyse biological literature and create databases. Avestha Gengraine, a life science company, has launched services in Bioinformatics segment with 60 people. Metahelix was another agri-biotech company that provides bioinformatics services. Strand Genomics is another active firm in this segment. IT majors like Wipro Technologies, Kshema Technologies, TCS and Satyam Computers have floated initiatives on bioinformatics by joining hands with biological laboratories, while Nicholas Piramal, a pharma major, has signed a deal with Delhi-based Centre for Biochemical Technology to collaborate on drug discovery. The major biotechnology service firms and their competence segments are given in Table 2.6.

Table 2.6: Major players in the service sector

Company Name	*Category*	*Technology*
Avesthagen	Contract research, Bioinformatics	Genomics, proteomics
Strand Genomics	Bioinformatics	—
Bangalore Genei	Contract research	Tool development for research
Genotypic Technology	Contract research, Bioinformatics	Nucleic acid (Contract Research)
Metahelix Life Sciences	Contract research	Tissue culture
DSQ Biotech	Contract research	Genomics
GVK Biosciences	Bioinformatics	—
Genomi Biotech	Contract research	DNA sequencing
Hitachi Genetech	Contract research	Genomics
iLabs	Bioinformatics	—
Nagarjuna Biotech	Contract research	Genomics
Kshema Technologies	Bioinformatics	—
Spectra Mind	Bioinformatics	—
Genequest	Contract research	Functional genomics
Biogen Technologies	Bioinformatics	—
Mahendra British Telecom	Bioinformatics	—
Nicholas Piramal	Bioinformatics	—
Syngene International	Bioinformatics	—
Ocimum Biosolutions Ltd.	Bioinformatics	—

Source: IBID data base and respective company profiles.

Bio-Suppliers

With many state governments attracting entrepreneurs and investors to invest in biotechnology, their focus has been on setting up biotechnology parks to provide basic infrastructure facilities like wet labs, incubators, centralized genomics, proteomics, chemistry, biology labs, bio-analytical lab, pre-clinical and clinical facilities, pilot plants to the up coming biotechnology companies. Apart from these facilities, biotech companies do need other regular items/equipments to carryout the routine operations. These have helped many MNCs to set up their subsidiaries to meet the requirements of the biotech companies.

Almost all the major players like Sartorius India, Millipore, Thermo Electron, Cambrex Chemicals, Amersham Biosciences, BioRad, Alfa Laval, Agilent, Kendro, Waters India and several other companies have set shop and are supplying equipments in large quantities in India. Besides, there are many companies in India like Span Diagnostics, Pharmalab, Praj Industries, Andel Equipment, Toshniwal Instruments, Ace Instruments, Biotech India, Bangalore Genie, Life Technologies, which are manufacturing the key equipments required for biotech companies. The facilitators like Sanjay Biotech, Biotech Suppliers and Services Network, Jain Biclogicals, Sigma Industrial and Laboratory Equipment, Life Technologies, and Fabtech Technologies are acting as distributors for equipments used for life sciences/biotechnology companies.

The suppliers are providing diverse products. Alfa Laval India supplies fermentor systems, CIP systems, heat exchangers, fittings, membrane filtration, bioreactors and mixing vessels. Ace Instruments supplies biological freezer, laboratory, pilot and industrial freeze dryers, bio-safety chambers; Span Diagnostics, supplies diagnostics reagents, instruments, accessories; Cambrex Chemicals sells cell biology and molecular biology products; Pall Pharmalab Filtration provides magnetic filter funnel and envirocheck sampling capsule (technologies), membrane and glass fiber filters, acrodisc syringe filter. The list is exhaustive.

There are about 25-40 key companies that are supplying equipment in India. Wipro is leading the race with total equipment sale of Rs. 78.45 crore followed by Millipore at Rs. 48.50 crore, and Agilent at Rs. 48 crore. The top five companies, Wipro, Millipore, Agilent, Becton Dickinson and Amersham account for over 55 percent market share. These equipment vendors are further gearing up expecting that a lot of biotech and life sciences companies will set up or upgrade their plants for getting FDA approvals.

Clustering and the Biotechnology Industry

Indian biotechnology firms are found to be mostly in six clusters. The industry is focused mainly in places like,

Bangalore, Hyderabad, Pune and Mumbai as shown in Figs. 2.3 and 2.4. Apart from Delhi and Chennai, Bangalore is ahead of other cities and is prompting convergence. Bangalore is strong in information technology and it is growing as a bioinformatics cluster and Hyderabad is the second largest cluster. All the major states in India are providing tax incentive programs for biotechnology companies and are investing in the construction of biotechnology research parks. The growth of biotechnology clusters can be attributed to four factors:

(1) The presence of excellent research capabilities in all these places which are capable of supporting infrastructure facility and provide highly experienced scientific talent. It can be seen from the Table 2.9 and 2.10 that many firms are associated with Indian Institute of Science, Bangalore and Center for Cellular and Molecular Biology, Hyderabad. The presence of strong research support is the main causal factor that created the clusters that act as knowledge networks, as shown by the Silicon Valley experience.

(2) The second factor is catalyzing the growth of biotechnology is the creation of biotechnology parks by various state governments.

(3) The third factor that catalyzed the growth of biotechnology is the entrepreneurial culture that spreads quickly and faster in clusters.

(4) The fourth element that catalyzed the growth of biotech firms is the availability of venture funds in the locations. There are about 70 funds operating in India. Most of venture supported firms are located in the four clusters.

SWOT Analysis of the Biotechnology Industry

Based on the data and growth trends, a detailed assessment of the strength, weakness, opportunities and threats analysis has been made. The major elements of strength have been, low operating cost, presence of good network, strong knowledge in basic sciences and rich biodiversity. From the opportunities side, biotech is a growth industry and India has a large pool of

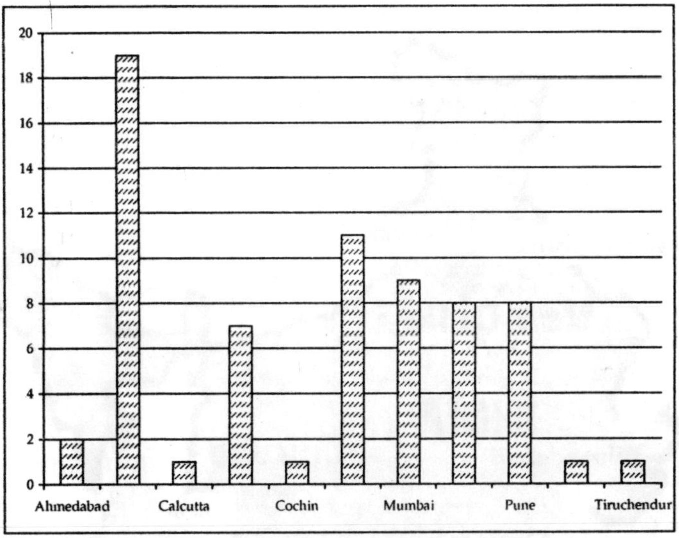

Source: Biospectrum

Fig 2.3: Biotechnology Clusters in India

talented scientists that can be exploited. The global biotech pipeline can be made rich, but currently it is lean. The strong IT base can be used for developing bioinformatics. There are many untouched areas in health care that can be exploited. There are a number of global players that are active in biotech research. They have strong brand valued products in the global market place. Indian biotech firms have to increase the level of R&D and create strong product portfolios. One of the major weaknesses that hamper the Indian biotech segment has been weakness of university system to contribute to new product or knowledge creation. This needs a serious policy consideration. However there are a number of weaknesses and threats that hamper the exploitation of the strengths, such as:

(1) Universities are not generating and transfer commercially exploitable knowledge. In the case of Silicon Valley, universities played a crucial role in creating new firms;

(2) The R&D expenditure by biotech firms are extremely low, compared to that in Israel, US, Ireland and France;

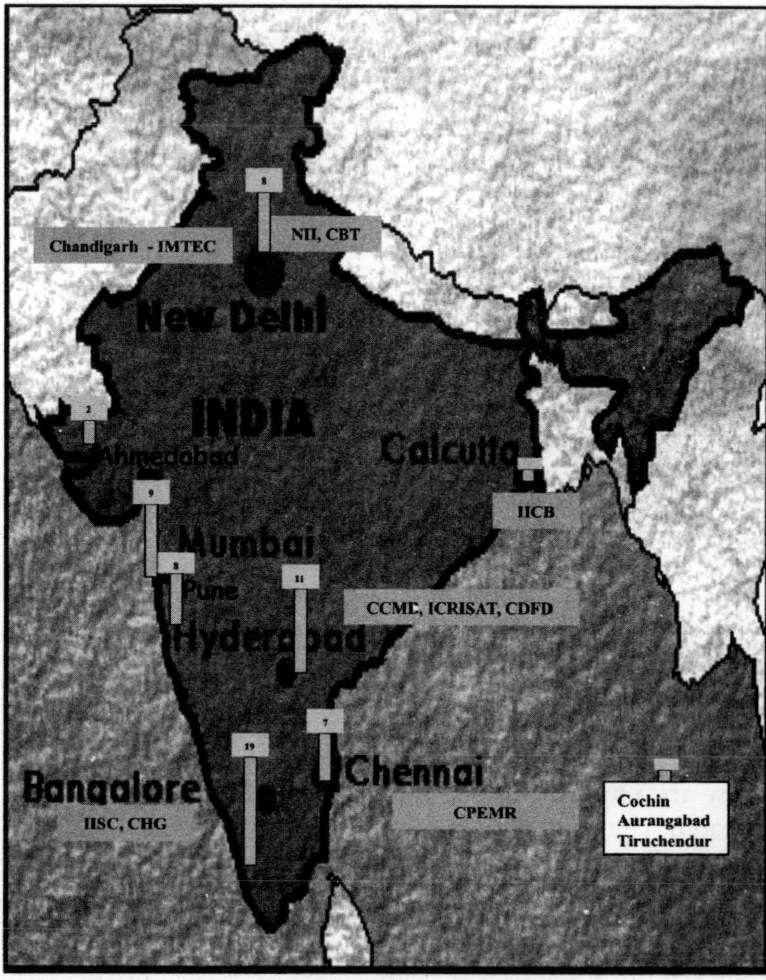

Fig 2.4: Biotechnology firms

(3) Indian biotechnology firms have to form links with firms that have strong product capability if they have to create value. Currently, they are focusing on biogenerics with low margins;

(4) Most of biotech firms are not cash rich firms that can invest in product development, as product development is a high-risk activity;

(5) Indian biotech firms are at the entry level and they have no experience at the operational level;
(6) The Indian biotech firms have no experience in taking new molecules through clinical trials; and
(7) Indian biotech firms have no major branded products for the global market.

Hence the SWOT analysis of Biotech industry is clearly shown in Figure 2.5.

Fig. 2.5: SWOT Analysis

Strength	*Weakness*
• Low operating cost • Good network of globally competitive research labs • Strong knowledge in basic sciences • Bio-diversity in human genome	• Missing link between research and commercialization • Low investment in R&D • Lack of alliances • Low value added products • Lack of financial resources for new firms • Many firms are at entry level • Lack of global experience • Lack of experience in clinical trials • Brand valued products for global market are less • Universities are weak in product creation
Opportunities	*Threats*
• Large pool of talented scientists • Global pipeline is close to empty • Strong IT base for bio informatics • Patent amendment after the year 2004 • Many untouched areas in health care	• Large number of global players • Strong brand valued products in global market

R&D Investments

The R&D expenditure of Indian biotechnology firms are low compared to the US or European biotechnology firms. The US biotechnology firms spend almost 29 percentage of their revenue on R&D. With the low levels of investments they are operating as shown in Table 2.7, and they will not be able to create any viable portfolio of products. The main weakness of Indian biotechnology segment is that neither the biotechnology firms nor the universities have demonstrated any significant new product creation capability. As biotechnology is an innovation based industry, absence of intellectual property will be a negative factor as far as India is concerned.

Table 2.7: R&D Expenditure pattern of major Indian biotechnology companies

Company name	*R&D spend 2001-02 (Rs. in million)*
Avesthagen	0.7
Bangalore Genei	1.4 (1.25% of Sales)
Genotypic Technology	0.4
Metahelix Life Sciences	1.0 (Not started generating revenue)
DSQ Biotech	0
Indfrag Biosciences	1.2
RPG Life Sciences	3.0 (0.09% of Sales)
Ajay Biotech	0.5 (1.82% of Sales)
A.V. Thomas Biotechnology	0
Spic	0
Bharat Biotech	3.6
Biological Evans	0
Bharat Immunological	0.75
Shantha Biotechnics	4.5
EID Parry (I) Ltd	29.7 (2.4% of Sales)
Basanth Agrotech (India) Ltd.	0.8 (0.20 % of Sales)

Source: IBID data base and respective company profiles.

Alliances

Biotechnology is a sector where the growth of strategic research alliances has been truly dramatic with over 20,000 alliances formed and has experienced an annual average growth rate of 2 per cent. The advent of biotechnology, the commercial application of recombinant DNA and molecular genetics technology was a marked departure from the chemically based expertise of the large firms and created the need for new collaborative research, joint ventures and new forms of cooperation [Feldman 2000]. There are five important factors in biotech research alliances, universities, small entrants, large biotech firms, large pharmaceutical firms, and research institutes. Universities and research institutes act as the source of scientific knowledge and talent, potentially important breakthroughs and intellectual property and access to the large number of patients required to complete clinical trials.

Essentially, Indian biotech firms are in its formative stage. They do not have extensive experience in drug discovery. The alliances of biotechnology firms can be broadly categorized into three groupings. The first category consists of alliances of Indian biotech firms and global research firms or institutions. This is emerging as a major group. This category of alliances are for research for new products, clinical trial and marketing of biotech products. The major alliances under this category are given in Table 2.8. The objective of this type of alliances can be termed value chain partnerships. The focus is to reduce the transaction cost and to enhance value addition. Risk sharing, pooling of resources and reducing the cycle time are some of the benefits of such alliances. As Indian firms do not have a product pipeline the motivation to enter into alliances are essentially to reduce the product development cycle time. The second category of alliances is between Indian contract research firms, bioinformatics and manufacturing firms and these are given in Table 2.9. These alliances have resulted in the formation of a bio-pharma-informatic networks. Many firms are entering into the biotech segments through alliances as they reduce the entry cost. The entry strategy of non-biotech firms have the third category of alliances is between firms and research labs. The major alliances of this type are given in Table 2.10. Through these alliances biotechnology networks are evolving. These alliances are also mostly occurring between institutes and firms. The glaring weakness one can observe from the information given in Table 2.10 is that universities are not active in biotech knowledge creation.

Table 2.8: Alliances between Indian firms and global firms

Name of the firm	*Alliance with*	*Nature of alliance*
Bharath Biotech Ltd	Centers for Disease Control-Atlanta (USA)	Malaria vaccine research
Reliance Life Sciences	United States Institutes of Health Research	Stem cell research
Wockhardt	Rhein Biotech	Tecomb HBSAg vaccine
Maharashtra Hybrid Seed Company Ltd (Mahyco)	Monsanto (U.S. based)	Genetically engineered cotton production
Questar	Alphaliene	Proteomics research
Nicholas Piramal	Cytran (USA)	Immunology, clinical trails, and marketing
Panacea	Chiron	Joint drug development
Strand Genomics	Metrigenix	Microarray technology sharing
Chembiotek	Bayer	Genomics
Indfrag Biosciences	Botanical Enterprises U.S.A.	Botanical extracts
Torrent	Sanofi (France)	R&D in healthcare products
Ub Group	Roussel Sante (France)	Recombinant insulin research
Ajay Biotech	Agro llogistics systems, U.S.A, Bio Grow Chemical, South Africa	Bio pesticides

Source: IBID data base and respective company profiles.

Table 2.9: Alliances between Indian contract research firms, bioinformatics and manufacturing firms

Name of the firm	*Alliance with*	*Nature of alliance*
GVK Biosciences	Ricerca LLC (USA)	Contract research
Bharat biotech	CDC (USA)	Clinical trial
Avesthagen	Genetic ID (U.S.A), Astrazeneca, ICRISAT	Contract Research
Genotypic Technologies	Quark Biotech Inc. USA QBI - Israel.	Bioinformatics
Syngene International	Strand genomics	Bioinformatics
CCMB	Satyam Computers	Bioinformatics

Source: IBID data base, respective company profiles.

Table 2.10: Major alliances between business firms and Government initiated Research institutes

Company name	*Alliance with*
Avesthagen	IISc. Bangalore
Bangalore Genei	IISc. Bangalore
Genotypic Technology	Astra Research Center, Bangalore IISc Bangalore, CCMB Hyderabad
Cadilla Pharmaceuticals	IISc Bangalore
Metahelix Life Sciences	IISc.. Bangalore
Bharat Petroleum Corp	TERI, New Delhi
Panacea Biotech	Centre for biotechnology, JNU Delhi
Shriram Biotech	Birla Institute of Scientific Research, Jaipur
Indian Immunologicals	Madras Veterinary College, Chennai
Zydus Cadilla Health Care	NIV Pune, IRR Mumbai
Bharat Biotech	CBT Delhi, CSIR Delhi, CCMB
Biological Evans	CCMB, University of Baroda
Shantha Biotech	CCMB, AIIMS, NII, IICB, JNU, Anna University

Source: IBID data base and respective company profiles.

Market Size and Output

Indian biotechnology industry output in 2002 was US $4 billion, which is 2 per cent share of the global market. The Indian industry is dominated by the health care segment accounting for 60 per cent of the share followed by industrial application, bioinformatics and genomics coming to 30 per cent and the remaining 10 per cent is agricultural Biotechnology. Not only that health care segment is large and it is growing rapidly compared to the other segments. Though agricultural biotechnology is critical for India, Indian firms are not active because of the weak regulatory system and low research intensity as well as the absence of focused research initiatives.

The output of domestic biotechnology industry is now estimated at $4 billion and it is likely to be about $20 billion in the next 10 years, as shown in Fig.2.1. The noticeable factor with Indian biotechnology industry is that majority of the firms are new (less than 5 year old) to the market and are located in five states namely Andhra Pradesh, Karnataka, Tamilnadu, Delhi and Maharastra. Two of the growing segments are contract research and bioinformatics. However, there are only a small number of firms, which are dedicated to molecular biotech products. Apart from this, only a very few manufacturing firms have collaborative programmes with foreign firms to produce new biotechnology products. One of the weaknesses observed is that the biotech firms do not have a robust product portfolio or a strong product pipeline that are likely to create blockbuster drugs.

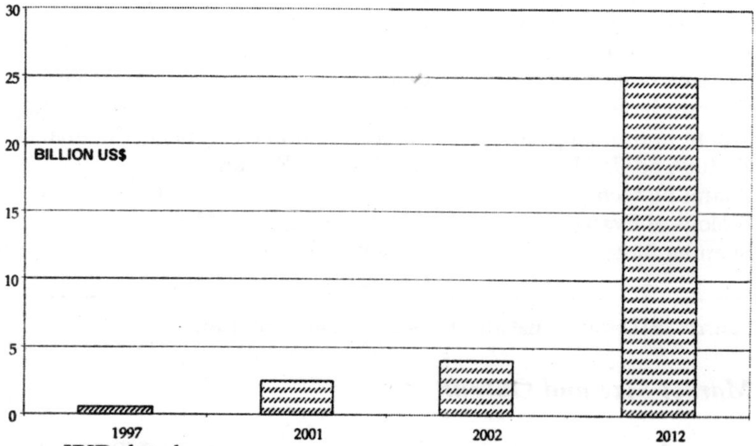

Source: IBID data base

Fig 2.6: Indian biotechnology market

The Future of Biotechnology Market in India

Indian Pharma industry is expected to grow to an innovation-led US $25 billion industry by 2010 with a market capitalization of almost US $150 billion from the current US $ 5 billion generic based drug industry. The vaccine market is expected to grow by roughly 20 per cent. India being the second largest food producer, offers a huge market for biotechnology products, especially agri-biotech products.

- India has an excellent scientific infrastructure in agriculture, rich bio-diversity and skilled and low cost human-power.

- In a report by Ernst and Young it is expected that the Nutraceuticals market is roughly US $532-638 million presently and growing.
- With its 8000 kilometer of coastline including Andaman and Nicobar and Lakshwadeep islands, India has a rich aqua culture and its Marine resource development holds great potential.

With increasing number of pharmaceutical companies finding it difficult to conduct entire drug discovery process-in-house they are looking for ways to minimize costs. India has become a very attractive base as the cost of infrastructure is relatively lower compared to other nations. Foreign companies also benefit from cheaper qualified workforce available in India. India produces enough qualified graduates each year thus companies looking to expand their operations can easily do so without facing a shortage in labour. Hence, the future of biotech in India in terms of market potentiality can be realized through the estimations of different organizations shown in Table 2.11.

Table 2.11: Differing Perspective on Biotech in India (2001)

	CII	*DBT*	*The Economist*
Biotech Market	$ 2.5 billion	$ 1,849 million	$ 1,475 Million
Agri/Seed Market	$ 500 million		$ 450 Million
Bio Informatics Market	$ 2.2 million		
Diagnostic/Vaccine Market	$ 420 million	$ 150 million	$ 375 Million

Source: RIS based on (i) Financial Express, 10th October, 2001, (ii) Business Standard, December 24th, 2000, (iii) Business line, July 9th, 2001, (iv) Economist, September 1st, 2001.

3

Policy Environment of Biotechnology Industry in India

Biotechnology, globally recognized as a rapidly emerging and far-reaching technology, is described as the "technology of hope" for its promising of food, health and environmental sustainability. The recent and continuing advances in life sciences clearly unfold a scenario energized and driven by the new tools of biotechnology. There are a large number of therapeutic biotech drugs and vaccines that are currently being marketed, which accounts for a US $40 billion market and benefiting over a hundred million people worldwide. In addition to these there are a large number of agri-biotech and industrial biotech products that have enormously helped mankind.

Human capital is perceived to be the key driver for global competitiveness. Added to this is a decreasing appetite for risk capital in developed countries, which has led to a decline in the biotechnology sector in these regions where survival lifelines are being provided by the lower cost research environs of the developing world such as India.

For a country like India, biotechnology is a powerful enabling technology that can revolutionize agriculture, healthcare, industrial processing and environmental sustainability. The Indian biotechnology sector has, over the last two decades, taken shape through a number of scattered and sporadic academic and industrial initiatives. The time is now ripe to integrate these efforts through a pragmatic National Biotechnology Development Strategy. It is imperative that the principal architects of this sector along with other key stakeholders play a concerted role in formulating such a strategy to ensure that we not only build on the existing platform but expand the base to create global leadership in biotechnology by unleashing the full potential of all that India has to offer.

Need for Biotechnology in India

Biotechnology can deliver the next wave of technological change that can be as radical and even more pervasive than that brought about by IT. Employment generation, intellectual wealth creation, expanding entrepreneurial opportunities, augmenting industrial growth are a few of the compelling factors that warrant a focused approach for this sector. Not only that, even to attract more benefits to the nation through new and potential technologies, government should play a strategic role. In this regard, potentiality of biotechnology in India should be explored as Indian Biotechnology sector is gaining global visibility and is being tracked for emerging investment opportunities.

This is the time for investment in frontier technologies such as biotechnology. It is envisaged that clearly thought-out strategies will provide direction and enable action by various stakeholders to achieve the full potential of this exciting field for the social and economic well being of the nation.

Vision and Mission

Biotechnology as a business segment for India has the potential of generating revenues to the tune of US$ 5 billion and creating one million jobs by 2010 through products and services. This can propel India into a significant position in the global biotech sweepstakes. Biopharmaceuticals alone have the potential to be a US$ 2 billion market opportunity largely driven by vaccines and bio-generics. Clinical development services can generate in excess of US$1.5 billion whilst bioservices or outsourced research services can garner a market of US$1 billion over this time scale. The balance US$500 million is attributable to agricultural and industrial biotechnology.

India has many assets in its strong pool of scientist and engineers, vast institutional network and cost effective manufacturing. There are over a hundred National Research Laboratories employing thousands of scientists. There are more than 300 college level educational and training institutes across the country offering degrees and diplomas in biotechnology, bio-informatics and the biological sciences, producing nearly 500,000 students on an annual basis. More than 100 medical colleges add ~17,000 medical practitioners per year. About 300,000 postgraduates and 1500 PhDs qualify in biosciences and engineering each year. These resources need to be effectively marshaled, championed and synergized to create a productive enterprise. India is reorganized as a mega bio-diversity country and biotechnology offers opportunities to convert our biological resources into economic wealth and employment opportunities. Innovative products and services that draw on renewable resources bring greater efficiency into industrial processes, check environmental degradation and deliver a more bio-based economy.

Indian agriculture faces the formidable challenge of having to produce more farm commodities for our growing human and livestock population from diminishing per capita arable land and water resources. Biotechnology has the potential to overcome this challenge to ensure the livelihood security of 110 million farming families in our country.

The advancement of biotech as a successful industry confronts many challenges related to research and development, creation of investment capital, technology transfer and technology absorption, patentability and intellectual property, affordability in pricing, regulatory issues and public confidence. Central to this are two key factors: affordability and accessibility to the products of biotechnology. Policies that foster a balance between sustaining innovation and facilitating technology diffusion need to be put in place.

There are several social concerns that need to be addressed in order to propel the emergence of biotechnology innovation in our country such as conserving bioresources and ensuring safety of products and processes. Government and industry have to play a dual role to advance the benefits of modern biotechnology while at the same time educate and protect the interests of the public. Wide utilization of new technologies would require clear demonstration of the new added value to all stakeholders.

The National Science and Technology Policy of the Government and the Vision Statement on Biotechnology issued by the Department of Biotechnology have directed notable interventions in the public and private sectors to foster life sciences and biotechnology. There has been substantial progress in terms of support for R&D, human resource generation and infrastructure development over the past decade. With the introduction of the product patent regime it is imperative to achieve higher levels of innovation in order to be globally competitive. The challenge now is to join the global biotech league.

This will require larger investments and an effective functioning of the innovation pathway. Capturing new opportunities and the potential economic, environmental, health and social benefits will challenge government policy, public awareness, educational, scientific, technological, legal and institutional framework.

The issue of access to the products arising from biotechnology research in both medicine and agriculture is of paramount importance. Therefore, there should be adequate support for public good research designed to reach the unreached in terms of technology empowerment. Both "public good" and "for profit" research should become mutually reinforcing. Public institutions and industry both have an important role in the process. The National Biotechnology Development Strategy takes stock of what has been accomplished and provides a framework for the future within which strategies and specific actions to promote biotechnology can be taken. The policy framework is a result of wide consultation with stakeholders—scientists, educationists, regulators, representatives of society and others and reflects their consensus. It focuses on cross-cutting issues such as human resource development academic and industry interface, infrastructure development, lab and manufacturing, promotion of industry and trade, biotechnology parks and incubators, regulatory mechanisms, public education and awareness building. This policy also aims to chalk out the path of progress in sectors such as agriculture and food biotechnology, industrial biotechnology, therapeutic and medical biotechnology, regenerative and genomic medicine, diagnostic biotechnology, bio-engineering, nano-biotechnology, bio-informatics and IT enabled biotechnology, clinical biotechnology, manufacturing and bio-processing, research services, bio-resources, environment and intellectual property and patent law. Several state governments have enunciated biotech policies spelling out a comprehensive blueprint for the sector. It is, therefore, prudent to have a National Biotech Development Strategy and policy that charts an integrated 10-year road map with clear directions and destinations.

Why and what should be Indian biotechnology policy?

Biotechnology has come to stay and will be a major technology of the future. Therefore, a biotechnology policy must plan for the future and any immediate expenditure on supporting biotechnology industry in a state and in the country must be regarded as an investment for the future which could bring unimagined returns.

It is, therefore, essential that our country needs a biotechnology policy. In fact, since ours is a large country with enormous diversity in every respect from state to state, it would be advisable for each state to have a biotechnology policy which would be in consonance with a larger, more flexible national biotechnology policy. As biotechnology is a hi-tech area. It requires substantial investment; yet it is labor intensive. It impinges on a variety of other areas, ranging from medicine and health to agriculture and industry. Its implications are many: social, economic, political, moral, ethical and legal. The biotechnology policy of the country defines the framework within which it is stated, areas where emphasis is to be laid, the kind of assistance and support that will be available from the government and how the responsibility for meeting the desired goals is intended to be assigned. The biotechnology policy must also state in detail the mechanism of its implementation and assessment by addressing the following issues:

- The importance, role and the scope of biotechnology.
- The world scenario and prospects in the various areas of biotechnology and many linkages of biotechnology with other areas of human endeavour.
- Basic requirements that need to be met in the various areas of biotechnology.
- The Indian advantage with special reference to the state concerned.
- What has been done in our country in each area.
- The chosen priorities and the rationale for them.
- The envisaged mechanism (in some detail) for achieving the priorities and how would the problems that may arise be overcome.
- The new institutions such as the biotech park, the new committees and the new funding agencies and their terms of reference.
- The time-frame for accomplishing the objectives.
- The role of the government, the institutions, the committees and the organizations involved.
- The mechanism of networking and monitoring, and
- An appropriate regulatory mechanism.

National Biotech Policy 2005

The biotechnology sector started to take shape in the country more than two decades ago. In the last five years, the biotechnology industry has really taken off and is about to cross the $1 billion mark, the country does not have a clearly defined policy framework for the biotech segment. The inaugural issue of BioSpectrum in March 2003 started the demand for a well-articulated National Biotechnology Policy. A year later, now there is a lot of action related to the formulation of a national policy for biotechnology. The government was all set to announce a national biotech policy in January 2005.

The government clearly recognizes that it is alive to the concerns of the industry as biotechnology has tremendous potential to resolve some basic issues like poverty, hunger and diseases which is very important to India. So the central aim of the Biotechnology Policy and Strategy would be towards full utilization of the potential of biotechnology for human welfare and economic development. For this, the policy would contain specific proposals and action points, incentives and programs. In addition to being a policy document, it would give a strategic direction to different sectors to accelerate the pace of development of biotechnology for the next ten years in the country. New models of center-state, private-public, R&D-industry partnership, inter ministerial, inter institutional/agency coordination would be worked on to exploit the full potential of the country in this sector.

Key Policy Recommendations and Interventions

Human Resource Development: Academic and Industry Needs

Biotechnology is a knowledge-driven technology, which needs to be driven by a flow of new ideas and concepts in the development of new tools for research, new processes for manufacturing and innovative business models.

The policy goal for the next decade is to facilitate the availability of scientific and technical human resource in all disciplines relevant to the life science and biotechnology sector. In order to build a successful biotechnology sector, large talent pools are required in multiple scientific disciplines such as molecular and cell biology, chemistry, physics, engineering, bioinformatics, medicine, agriculture, microbiology, technology transfer and commercialization, bioentreprise and biofinancing and intellectual property rights management. Product and process development are inter-disciplinary in nature and deficiencies in specific areas may weaken the whole sector. The key issue is the manner in which to create an effective interface across disciplines.

Reliable estimates of human resource availability for the next 10 years are required. Expert consensus indicates that there is adequate enrollment currently at the post-graduate and under-graduate levels, however the quality is inconsistent. Areas such as intellectual property rights, regulatory issues and industrial training have received inadequate attention. There is a consensus that there is an urgent need to augment the number of Ph.D. programs in the Life Sciences and biotechnology. A strong pool of academic leaders is key to sustained innovation.

Strategic Actions

(i) National Task Force on Education and Training

- A National Task Force will be created to formulate model undergraduate and postgraduate curricula in Life Sciences keeping in view, future needs. The said curricula must address the underlying need for multi-disciplinary and inter-disciplinary learning and the appropriate stage for biotechnology training.

(ii) Need Assessment

- There would be need assessment in 2005 for the next five years and close monitoring during the period for interim changes.
- A 10-year perspective plan for human resource will be prepared every five years.

(iii) Curriculum Development

- Course curricula will be reviewed and improved in consultation with industry and research establishments and standard e-learning modules will be developed for specific skill areas such as IPR, regulations, and bioentreprise.
- Hands on exposure to M.Sc. biotechnology students will be enhanced through an extended industry internship as well as through short-term placements at CSIR and other appropriate National Institutes.
- Dual degree programs in biotechnology that include regulatory matters, IPR and bio-enterprise management will be encouraged and supported by the Department of Biotechnology.
- Emphasis will be given on training of high quality technicians and technologists in skills required by the industry by establishing Regional training centres at diploma, graduate and postgraduate levels.

(iv) Quality Improvement

- An accreditation mechanism will be put in place for ensuring minimum standard of education and training at the post-graduate and undergraduate levels. Base requirements for teaching and laboratory infrastructure will be specified and enforced.
- Teachers training programs will be taken up by creating regional teachers training centres.

(v) Strengthening of teaching and R&D in life sciences and biotechnology in the university system

- Strengthening R&D in Life Sciences and biotechnology in the university system will be accorded high priority. This is considered important for improving the quality of education and providing exposure to new technologies for students at various levels. Specific mechanisms to achieve the goal will include:

  (1) Creation of inter-disciplinary centres of excellence with world class infrastructure in key areas,
  (2) Program support to encourage inter-departmental networking,
  (3) Visiting professorship and creation of industry sponsored chairs in partnership with the Department of Biotechnology.

(vi) Attracting talent to life science and biotechnology

Bright students will be attracted to take up careers in biology and biotechnology through special scholarships. Summer assignments at Academic and Industry research laboratories will be introduced at the school level to create interest in the fields of biotechnology and biology. Women scientists will be encouraged to take up careers in biotechnology. Service conditions will be liberalized for women to be able to return to research/academics after maternity breaks.

(vii) Creating science and technology leaders for the industry

- The number of Ph.D fellowships offered by the Department of Biotechnology will be increased to 200 per annum.

- Public-private partnerships will be encouraged in Ph.D. programs through creation of the *'Bio-edu-Grid'*- a network of universities and industries facilitating pooling of resources.
- Masters degree level professionals in industry will be encouraged to undertake Ph.D. programs while retaining their jobs through industry-university tie-ups.

(viii) Arresting and reversing brain drain

- As mentioned earlier, the number of postdoctoral fellowships offered by the Department of Biotechnology will be increased to 200 per annum in order to attract talent.
- Outstanding young investigator grants in biotechnology will be introduced. This will provide a package including salary support, research grant, equipment and opportunities to attend national and international conferences. The salary support under the scheme will be at par with that of entry-level faculty positions.
- Information on availability of positions in education/ research establishments and industries will be provided on a website to facilitate employment of scientists with specific skills at appropriate positions.
- A database of scientists working in different areas of biotechnology within and outside the country will be created to utilize the expertise appropriately.

Enabling working conditions for scientists to undertake industry oriented research

Lateral mobility of scientific personnel: Scientists working at universities and research institutions may be allowed to work in industries for commercialization of their research efforts. This could be in the form of secondment or consultancy with industry or by a sabbatical for three years during the working life of scientists.

Dual/adjunct faculty positions: Researchers working in university/research institutions may be allowed to hold positions in the industry and vice-versa.

Joint salary support: Faculty employed in academic institutions may be allowed to hold positions for a period of time in which their salary is contributed both by the industry and the academic institution on a mutually agreed basis. (Such an arrangement will work well only if the teaching requirements of the academic institutions are made obligatory).

Rapid travel grants: Rapid travel grants scheme for approval within two weeks for young scientists to interact with mentors and industry collaborators would be initiated.

Institute Innovation Grants: Through the Department of Biotechnology to fund academic researchers to develop their concepts into patentable and more importantly licensable technologies. These steps will ensure that the large available resources of human talent in biotechnology are supported and this will guarantee the progress of the biotech sector.

Infrastructure Development and Manufacturing

The strength of a biotechnology company lies in up scaling a number of proven technologies—diagnostics, vaccines, products, and processes—for fine-tuning and large-scale production. While Indian industry is strong in product development and marketing for commercial benefits, biotechnology in India still lacks the infrastructure required to take up R&D in areas like molecular modeling, protein engineering, drug designing, immunological studies, pre-clinical studies, clinical trials, etc.

In order to get the best from public and privately funded biological/biotechnological research, it is imperative to utilize the infrastructure generated optimally for societal benefits. The concept of Contract Research Organizations (CROs), Contract Manufacturing Organizations (CMOs), contract packagers, lab services providers etc., is steadily taking shape in India. In the area of biomanufacturing, industry estimates that the market for biogenerics in India is expected to see a 43 per cent jump from Rs. 308.50 crore in 2001 to Rs. 1,305.7 crore in 2005 and projected to reach Rs. 1,864.3 crore by 2007 registering a growth of 19 per cent.

India's strengths lie in the availability of educated and skilled manpower, proficiency in English, low capital and operational costs and the proven track record in meeting international standards of quality. There is ample proof that the Indian companies are committed to global standards. According to reports, outside of the US, India ranks the highest with 61 USFDA-approved plants and in excess of 200 GMP certified pharmaceutical manufacturing facilities.

Strategic Actions

(i) Department of Biotechnology will act to facilitate a Single Window Clearance mechanism for establishing Biotechnology plants.
(ii) Encourage private participation in infrastructure development like roads, water supply and effluent treatment.
(iii) Depositories of biological materials will be created in partnership with industry on IDA model for agriculturally important organisms, medically important organisms, plasmids, cosmids and constructs of special nature generated with adequate human interventions.
(iv) State of the art large animal house facilities with GLP will be created for testing candidate vaccines and biotherapeutics. Testing facilities will be created for GMO/LMO.

Promotion of Industry and Trade

The emergence of India as a global player in the biotech sector requires government to play the role of a champion and foster an international competitive environment for investment and enterprise development. India's strategy must be to get more value from its R&D investment and from IPR generation. The current policy review envisages an annual turnover of US$ 5 billion by 2010. India has to develop its own biotechnological and pharmaceutical products to ensure quality and affordability for global trade. In addition to opportunities in drug discovery and development there are significant openings to provide services to the worldwide biotech and pharmaceutical industries and to leverage low cost high quality manufacturing with a global discovery potential. Capitalizing on these opportunities would create many new valuable jobs in India as we have seen in the outsourcing and service industry.

In a highly competitive and fast moving business environment, innovative capacity is an important determinant of the ability to create a continuing pipeline of new products and processes. Innovation covers knowledge creation (R&D), knowledge diffusion (education and training) and knowledge application (commercialization). Innovation is not a one-time event; instead, it has to continuously respond to changing circumstances for creating sustainable growth. Innovation is measured in terms of external/domestic patent applications; human capital devoted to R&D, government expenditure on R&D proportionate to country's GDP, business funded expenditure on R&D, indigenous technologies standardized, demonstrated and transferred to industry for commercialization; and the number of spin off companies created. Government policies for promotion of innovation and commercialization of knowledge will propel the growth of the biotechnology sector:

Strategic Actions

- Basic and translational research in key biological processes and new materials will be supported as innovation for tomorrow. Access to the knowledge generated will be improved by supporting knowledge and social networks among stakeholders so that those with appropriate skills can convert the research output into useful products and processes.
- Research to promote innovation must be supported increasingly on a cooperative rather than a competitive basis. This requires effective communication among

science agencies, research institutions, academia and industry.

- To promote India as a hub of innovation, a network of relevant stakeholders should be developed. Public investment should be used as a catalyst to promote such clustering and networking as this can lead to enhance creativity by sharing of expertise, resources and infrastructure.
- Availability of human resource would be ensured at each phase of the product cycle.
- Strengthening technology transfer capacity.

It is proposed to create several national/regional technology transfer cells (TTC's) over the next 5 years to provide high caliber, specialized and comprehensive technology transfer services. The services would include: evaluating technology and identifying potential commercial uses, developing and executing and intellectual property protection strategies identifying potential licensees and negotiating licenses. Each TTC would service a cluster of institutions in a region or a large city. Optimal delivery of services by the TTCs requires professionals with background in industry and science, wide networks, an external focus and high level licensing skills. The best practices for effective technology transfer will be benchmarked.

The skills of existing technology transfer professionals will be upgraded by a combination of specialized training courses, including linking to important programs redesigning the incentives and career paths for posting. Scientists and other innovators shall be equipped with a better understanding of markets and commercialization pathways, the process of technology transfer, the strategy of protecting intellectual property rights and industrial licensing.

Fiscal and trade policy initiatives

Biotechnology firms are by and large research intensive among major industries. On an average the biotechnology sector invests 20-30 per cent of its operating costs in R&D or technology outsourcing. Government support, fiscal incentives and tax benefits are therefore critical to this sector. These measures will also help to capitalize on the inherent cost effectiveness of the Indian biotech enterprise. The suggested interventions include:

- Exemption of import duties on key R&D, contract manufacturing/clinical trial equipment and duty credit for R&D consumer goods to enable small and medium entrepreneurs to reduce the high capital cost of conducting research.
- Extending the 150 per cent weighted average tax deduction on R&D expenditure under section 35 (2AB) until 2010 and to permit international patenting costs under this provision and enable eligibility of expenditure incurred with regard to filing patents outside India for weighted deductions u/s 35 (2 AB)
- Enable lending by banks to biotech companies as priority sector lending. Currently banks are almost averse to lending to young biotech companies. In order to encourage banks to lend and provide banking services to the biotech sector, a significant push through appropriate policy guidelines from the Reserve Bank of India is necessary. Currently lending to agri-businesses as well as investment in Venture Funds by banks is categorized as Priority Sector Lending. Biotech as a business has similar characteristics in terms of risk as well as gestation time lines and it is therefore recommended that lending to Biotech be also categorized as Priority Sector lending.
- Remove customs duty on raw materials imported into India, where the finished product is imported duty free. Life Saving Drugs imported and sold in India are exempted from paying customs duty; whereas raw materials for diagnostics and other pharmaceutical biotech products manufactured in India are levied customs duty. To promote the indigenous

manufacturing industry and make it competitive globally, raw materials imported by Indian manufacturers should be eligible for Duty Drawback.

- Rationalization of import and export of biological material is considered critical for clinical research and business process outsourcing.
- Simplification and streamlining of procedures for import, clearance and storage of biologicals, land acquisition, obtaining environmental and pollution control approvals would be simplified and streamlined within shorter time frame lines through consultations with various central and state government departments.
- As an effective regulatory mechanism has been put in place though recent interventions, Foreign Investment Promotion Board (FIPB) approval for equity investment may no longer be necessary.
- Joint R&D collaboration and generation of joint IP though global partnerships would be fostered.
- International trade opportunities would be promoted to guide R&D investment Indian biotech strengths would be aggressive by promoted globally.
- Efforts would be made to remove hurdles for contract research especially for input output norms and tax on revenue generated through contract research/R&D.
- Easy access to information, regarding legislation and rules and regulations for transboundary movements of biologicals would be promoted.
- Current standards and safety of products would be enhanced.
- Efforts would be strengthened to promote acceptance of Indian regulatory data internationally.
- Research, trade and industrial partnership would be fostered at regional and sub-regional levels.
- A "cluster" approach would be encouraged to operations. One significant features of the industry is the fluidity and variety of its inter-company relationships, traditionally much greater than in other

industries. It has relied to a considerable degree on contracting and outsourcing, especially "upstream" in R&D through various licensing arrangements and "downstream" through co-marketing agreements.

- Collaborative knowledge networks would be promoted. Expanded sharing of information, including creation/use of collaborative knowledge networks (CKN), can greatly enhance a company's performance under a cluster approach. Managing the many external relationships is complex. Flexible and pervasive communications systems that allow information to flow effortlessly within and between contracting organizations will provide the key to success. Increasingly, IT advances, including web-based approaches, will provide the foundation for these systems.

Public investment for promotion of innovation and knowledge commercialization

Availability of financial support for early phase of product development to establish proof-of-principle is the key to sustaining innovation. In this context, it is proposed to institute *'Small Business Innovation Research Initiative'* (SBIRI) scheme through the Department of Biotechnology in 2005-06 for supporting small and medium size enterprises as a grant/loan. Companies with up to 1000 employees will be eligible. The scheme will support pre-proof of concept, early stage innovative research and provide mentorship and problem solving support in addition to the grant/soft loan. The SBIRI scheme will operate in two phases of innovation and product development.

SBIRI Phase-I

The funding in this stage will be provided for highly innovative, early stage, pre-proof-of-concept research. Preference will be given to proposals that address important national needs. The maximum amount of funding to an enterprise will be limited to Rs. 50 lakh with not more than 50 per cent of it going as grant and the remaining as an interest free loan. For projects to be considered at this stage, though a partner from a public R&D institution would be considered important, it will not be a mandatory requirement for those companies that have good quality scientists. This should encourage high quality scientists to agree to work in small and medium biotech companies, a change from our traditions. The R & D requirement of the public institution will be met through a grant.

SBIRI Phase-II

It is expected that some of the proposals funded with SBIRI Phase-I will establish the proof-of-concept. At this stage, the ability of the project to get venture capital funding improves. Such projects will be eligible for Phase-II funding. Some projects could be eligible for direct phase-II support. It is proposed to provide soft loan at this stage for product development and commercialization at an interest rate of 2 per cent. The role of public R&D institution at this stage too is critical. The partner in the public institution at this stage will get the R&D support as grant. Small and medium knowledge-based industries in biotech sector will be encouraged to avail of equity support from the SME Growth Fund of Small Industries Development Bank of India (SIDBI).

Code of best practice for disclosure guidelines

Setting up a 'Code for Best Practice for Disclosure Guidelines for the Indian Biotech Industry'. This Code will be a part of the General Listing Requirements and Disclosure Guidelines and will be in conjunction with SEBI's General Listing Rules and Disclosure Guidelines.

Biotechnology Parks and Incubators

Establishing biotechnology parks for the growth of the biotechnology industry is essential either through public-private alliance or public/private sponsorships. With its large human resource in molecular biology, microbiology, biochemical engineering, synthetic organic chemistry, chemical engineering and allied branches of engineering and strong institutional base at the universities, CSIR, ICMR and ICAR, India is well placed to support a number of biotech parks.

Biotechnology Parks can provide a viable mechanism for licensing new technologies to upcoming biotech companies to start new ventures and to achieve early stage value enhancement of the technology with minimum financial inputs. These biotech parks facilitate the lab to land transfer of the technologies by serving as an impetus for entrepreneurship through partnership among innovators from universities, R&D institutions and industry.

Basic minimum components for parks should include research laboratories for product development, multi-purpose pilot facility for manufacturing and process development, quality control and validation of technologies, common effluent treatment plant, a GLP Animal House, a recognized human resource training centre, administrative support centre etc.

The biotech parks should be located so as to be easily accessible for all the stakeholders, tenants, academia with connecting roads, water and power supply and should also attract less administrative clearances from the government.

Strategic Actions

(i) The Department of Biotechnology will promote and support at least 10 biotech parks by 2010. Each park will necessarily meet the qualifying criteria related to the characteristics of the location, a viable business plan, management strategy and a clear definition of the partners and their roles.

(ii) The Department of Biotechnology will support creation of incubators in biotech parks promoted by a private industry or through public-private partnership in the form of grant upto 30 per cent of the total cost or upto 49 per cent in the form of equity.

(iii) It is proposed that a central body *Biotechnology Parks Society of India (BPSI)* be set up for the promotion of biotechnology parks in the country on the same lines of the Software Technology Parks of India (STPI). The BPSI should be run by professionals having experience in the areas of biotechnology, knowledge in Acts and Rules relevant to biotechnology and management skills. The existing parks can become members of these new biotech parks. The BPSI would be responsible for evaluating the project proposals and advising the Department of Biotechnology on the funding pattern; facilitating industries in obtaining industrial, environmental and other relevant approvals from the central government; making recommendation regarding fiscal incentives to be granted to the biotechnology parks; providing guidance to the venture capital institutions on investment in biotech parks; providing accreditation to the parks etc.

(iv) Concessions to biotech companies located in biotech parks: Biotech companies located at biotech parks are eligible for benefits as per the recent changes in the Foreign Trade Policy:

- Duty free import of equipment, instruments and consumables.
- Tax holiday under Section 10A/10B of the Income Tax Act.
- A scheme will be put in place for operationalising of the incentives to biotech units located in biotech parks. As a part of this scheme biotech company located in biotech parks to be allowed a five-year time frame to meet the export obligation norms under the SEZ scheme. This measure helps to address the long and unpredictable gestational time lines that are inherent to biotech product development.

Regulatory Mechanisms

It is important that biotechnology is used for the social benefit of India and for economic development. To fulfil this vision, it has to be ensured that research and application in biotechnology is guided by a process of decision-making that safeguards both human health and the environment with adherence to the highest ethical standards. There is consensus that existing legislation, backed by science based assessment procedures clearly articulates rules and regulations that can efficiently fulfil this vision. Choices are required to be made that reflect an adequate balance between benefit, safety, access and the interest of consumers and farmers. It is also important that biotechnology products that are required for social and economic good are produced speedily and at the lowest cost. A scientific, rigorous, transparent, efficient, predictable, and consistent regulatory mechanism for biosafety evaluation and release system/protocol is an essential for achieving these multiple goals.

Strategic Actions

(i) The recommendation of the Swaminathan Committee on regulation of agri-biotech products and of the Mashelkar Committee on recombinant pharma products will be implemented in 2005.

(ii) It is recommended that an event that has already undergone extensive biosafety tests should not be treated as a new event if it is in a changed background containing the tested and biosafety evaluated "event". Where adequate evidence is available that the recurrent parent genetic background of a notified/registered genotype is nearly restored (through field data/ molecular data), only the agronomic performance and the level and stability of the transgene expression may be analyzed by two-year trial data by the ICAR. Even in case of a structurally altered transgene with no significant modifications in protein conformation, the toxicity and allergenicity tests need not be carried out provided the predicted antigenic epitope remains the same and the level of expression of the transgene is within the defined limits. For the released event, Department is of the view that there is no need of large-scale trials under the Genetic Engineering Approval Committee, as the biosafety aspects have been already addressed adequately before releasing the "event". Only ICAR trials may address the agronomic evaluation of the crop.

(iii) An inter-ministerial group chaired by a reputed scientist will be established in 2005 to address anomalies and issues that arise in regulation from time to time. It is proposed that the administrative support to this committee be through the Department of Biotechnology. The mandate of the committee should be to vet any changes in policies, procedures, protocols by departments dealing with regulation in biotech products and processes; resolve issues emanating from the overlapping/conflicting rules in various acts related to regulation of biotechnology activities in R&D, import, export, releases etc. and to review guidelines, protocols, standard operating procedures and ensure their dissemination to all stakeholders from time to time.

(iv) A competent single National Biotechnology Regulatory Authority be established with separate divisions for agriculture products/transgenic crops, pharmaceuticals/drugs and industrial products; and transgenic food/feed and transgenic animal/aqua-culture. The authority is to be governed by an independent administrative structure with common chairman. The inter-ministerial group will evolve suitable proposals for consideration of the government.

(v) A centre for in-service training of all professionals, irrespective of their location, engaged in the regulatory process to be established by the Department of Biotechnology in close collaboration with other concerned departments and institutions.

(vi) All existing guidelines to be updated and made consistent with the recommendations of the Swaminathan and Mashelkar Committees in 2005. New guidelines on transgenic research and product/process development in animal, aqua-culture, food, phyto-pharma and environmental application to be put in place in 2005 by the concerned ministries/departments

(vii) As an interim measure, a special regulatory cell will be created by the DBT to build capacity in the country for scientific risk assessment, monitoring and management, to foster international linkages, support biosafety research; to obtain and review feedback from different stakeholders and provide support to industry and R&D institutions. This cell will only have a promotional and catalytic role.

(viii) Measures will be taken to build professionalism and competence in all agencies involved with regulation of biotechnology products.

(ix) Research is support of regulation, to safeguard health and environment shall be supported by the concerned funding agencies to generate knowledge that will guide regulations and bioethics policy.

(x) Concerned ministries will make a vigorous effort to promote acceptance of the Indian regulatory decisions by other trading countries.

Public Communication and Participation

Biotechnology today has become as important as traditional plant and animal breeding have been in the past. At the same time, it raises a number of difficult economic, social, ethical, environmental and political issues that constitute major challenges for the human society. The reception of biotech products by the public has been rather mixed. In general biopharmaceutical products seem to be better accepted than transgenic crops. Clearly it is no longer possible to assume automatic public acceptance of new products and processes that promise public and commercial benefits. Public perception and opinion have a significant influence on the direction and funding of biotechnology research. Hence there is a need to work actively and transparently to inform and engage the civic society in decision-making, and to maintain a relationship of trust and confidence. The government and the industry must actively promote access to information on the benefits and risks in a balanced manner.

To achieve this goal, several enabling factors already exist: a sound biosafety regulatory system; well respected appellate and judicial system for redressal of grievances; cadre of willing and able scientists for effective and accurate communication of information; a large body of extension personnel in agriculture, fisheries, veterinary and human health sectors; large NGO network spread across the country; and an effective and independent mass media.

However, several challenges to success need to be recognized while framing the strategies; they are: diverse levels of education and literacy across the country; low understanding of biotechnology among the public; lack of simple communication material; varying quality of science reporting; inadequate inter agency coordination; insufficient dialogue between scientists, industry, policy makers, regulators, consumer for a civil society organizations and the mass media; and lack of sufficiently proactive administrative machinery.

There is a need to build public awareness about opportunities and challenges presented by biotechnology development and to inspire public trust and confidence on the safety, efficacy as well as social and ethical acceptability of products among consumers and civil society through the dissemination of accurate information in a coherent, balanced well articulated, user-friendly and transparent manner. Several focused and well-directed measures are needed to achieve public trust and confidence in biotechnology.

Strategic Actions

(i) Create a cadre of resource persons to reach the stakeholders

- Creation of a cadre of resource persons to provide credible information based on scientific data,
- Training media personnel through Institutes of Mass Communication, colleges of journalism and others,

- Capacity building among extension personnel in agricultural, fisheries, veterinary and medical sectors,
- Involvement of *Panchayati Raj Institutions* in the process of analysis and understanding the risks and benefits associated with GMOs as they will be playing an important role in the local level management of bio-diversity, access to benefit sharing etc.
- Awareness generation among undergraduate and post-graduate students in universities, colleges etc. on issues related to biosafety,
- Promoting a genetic literacy movement within government and public schools through 50 genome clubs nature clubs each year.

(ii) Creating a media resource network

- To facilitate access to information.

(iii) Empowering policy makers

- Regular training programs for policy-makers.

(iv) Empowering the judiciary

- Setting up a training school for the judiciary under the aegis of Centre for DNA Fingerprinting and Diagnostics, Hyderabad,
- Training through the National Law Schools and other similar institutions,

(v) Institutional mechanisms for strengthening public trust

- Establishment of a dedicated training centre for biosafety, food and nutrition safety and standards as per codex alimentarius committee.
- Creation of a 'National Biotechnology Awareness Fund' for providing support for the education and preparation of educational resource material for various sections of stakeholders in different regional languages of the country.

About Government of Andhra Pradesh

Government of Andhra Pradesh has identified the biotech sector as one of the "Engines of Growth" in the Vision 2020 document. The Government will leverage the existing strengths of the State for rapid commercialization of biotechnology to produce innovative biotech products and services in a wide range of areas.

The Government of Andhra Pradesh recognizes the pioneering efforts made by a few entrepreneurs in setting up highly successful biotech companies such as, Shanta Biotechnics, Ltd. and Bharat Biotech Ltd. which have, in a very short span of time, gained world-wide recognition and put Andhra Pradesh in the forefront of the Biotech revolution in India. The Government envisages a very active role of the private sector in the development of the biotechnology industry.

The Government would act as a facilitator and a catalyst. It has felt the need for a well-defined policy to forge a Private-Public Partnership in the development of biotechnology in the State. It is expected that the large number of scientists from Andhra Pradesh, who are at present engaged in research, academics or manufacturing in the field of biotechnology in USA and other developed countries will play catalytic and enabling role in developing biotechnology in the State, given the right environment, as was the case with Information Technology.

The objectives of the Biotech Policy are:

(1) To take up a detailed inventory of the bio-resources in the State with the help of Universities, research institutions, NGOs and private agencies.
(2) To promote conservation of bio-diversity and sustainable exploitation of bio-resources.
(3) To create a congenial environment for encouraging R&D in biotechnology and allied fields through the development of infrastructure and through appropriate incentives and regulatory framework for research.
(4) To develop high quality infrastructure with the required support services for manufacturing units by setting up specialized Biotech Parks in various parts of the State.

(5) To provide special incentives to the biotech industry and related sectors to focus on human resource development in the area.

(6) To create an enabling environment for the growth of the biotech industry, especially the simplification of procedures for getting clearances for the commercialization of new biotech products and for the use of laboratory animals for drug discovery.

(7) To develop bioinformatics, leveraging the State's existing strength in Information Technology for the development of biotechnology.

(8) To facilitate the flow of venture capital funds and bank credit to biotech companies.

(9) To address issues such as Intellectual Property Rights, Biosafety, Bio-surveillance and Bio-ethics.

4

Government Funding of Biotechnology

Institutional Setup and Budgetary Allocations

India is one of the first few countries, among the developing countries, to have recognized the importance of biotechnology as a tool to advance growth of agricultural and health sectors as early as in 1980s. India's Sixth Five Year Plan (1980-85) was the first policy document to cover biotechnology development in the country. The plan document proposed to strengthen and develop capabilities in areas such as immunology, genetics, communicable diseases, etc. In this context, referring to the Council of Scientific and Industrial Research (CSIR), the document suggested to ensure coordination on inter-institutional, inter-agency and on multi-disciplinary basis, full utilization of existing facilities and infrastructure in major areas including biotechnology. Programmes in the area of biotechnology included, tissue culture application for medicinal and economic plants, fermentation technology and enzyme engineering for chemicals, antibiotics and other medical product development; agricultural and forest residues and slaughterhouse wastes utilization and emerging areas like genetic engineering and molecular biology.

The existing national laboratories under the S&T agencies, such as Indian Council of Medical Research (ICMR) and Council for Scientific and Industrial Research (CSIR) had initiated several research programmes to fulfil the above plan objectives. At the top, an apex official agency viz. National Biotechnology Board (NBTB) was set up in 1982, to spearhead development of biotechnology. The NBTB was chaired by Member (Science) of the Indian Planning Commission and had representation of almost all the S&T agencies in the country viz. Department of Science and Technology (DST), Council for Scientific and Industrial Research (CSIR), Indian Council of Agricultural Research (ICAR), Indian Council for Medical Research (ICMR), Department of Atomic Energy (DAE) and the University Grants Commission (UGC). NBTB was formed with the specific purpose of the identification of priority areas and for evolving a long-term plan for the country in biotechnology as well as to initiate and promote such activities as conducive for further development of various areas in biotechnology. The NBTB issued the *"Long Term Plan in Biotechnology for India"* in April 1983, which document spelt out priorities for biotechnology in India in view of the national objectives such as self-sufficiency in food, clothing and housing, adequate health and hygiene, provision of adequate energy and transportation, protection of environment, gainful employment, industrial growth and balance in international trade. Later in 1986, NBTB graduated to a full-fledged government department called Department of Biotechnology (DBT).

At present in India, there are six major agencies responsible for financing and supporting research in the realm of biotechnology apart from other sciences. They are Department of Science and Technology (DST), Department of Biotechnology (DBT), Council of Scientific and Industrial Research (CSIR), Indian Council of Medical Research (ICMR), Indian Council of Agriculture Research (ICAR) and University Grants Commission (UGC), Department of Scientific and Industrial Research (DSIR). DST, DBT and DSIR are part of Ministry of Science and Technology while ICMR is with Ministry of Health, ICAR with Ministry of Agriculture and UGC with Ministry of Human Resource and Development. DSIR is the funding agency for CSIR and both of them independently fund biotechnology related research programmes.

As Table 4.1 shows the allocations for all of these agencies have gone up in the last decade. Out of this, DBT is the only agency completely devoted to R&D in biotechnology. It is very difficult to estimate the total allocations for this sector *per se* from other aforementioned agencies as in some cases the allocations are not separately marked as allocations for biotechnology. One faces this kind of constraint especially with those organizations, which are focusing on technological solutions and are not committed for X or Y nature of technology. Thus separately accounting for biotechnology becomes difficult. It would probably become possible only if a detailed survey at the institutional level is undertaken. Table 4.1 gives a broad idea about total allocations by major Indian funding agencies to science and technology related projects and not necessarily to biotechnology alone. In case of UGC it gives a broad idea not only about S&T related projects but also about other research streams.

Table 4.1: Budgetary Allocations of Major Funding Agencies in India (Rs. Million)

	1990/91	*2000/01*
Department of Scientific and Industrial Research (DSIR)	131.3	583.8
Department of Science and Technology (DST)	2588.9	7798
Department of Biotechnology (DBT)	655	1361
Indian Council of Agriculture Research (ICAR)	3236	13990
Indian Council of Medical Research (ICMR)	396	1470
Council of Scientific and Industrial Research (CSIR)	2351	9120
University Grants Commission (UGC)	3495	14070

Source: RIS based on budgetary papers of relevant years, Ministry of Finance, Government of India.

Department of Biotechnology (DBT)

Recognizing the importance of biotechnology, in India in 1981, the government established a National Biotechnology Board (NBTB). In 1986, the NBTB was replaced by the Department of Biotechnology (DBT) and was given the primary responsibility for the promotion of the biotechnology at all levels. In 1990, the need to have an institutional mechanism to ensure close interaction between research and development, pilot plant studies, market survey, certification and technology developments has led to the creation of the Biotech Consortium India Limited (BCIL, 1990).

Under the auspices of the Scientific Advisory Committee of the DBT, thirteen Task Forces were constituted which covered practically all the important disciplines of biotechnology, including manpower development. More than 200 researchers, drawn from university departments, national laboratories, industries and governmental organizations, are involved in identifying new areas as well as upgrading modifying the ongoing programmes. The essential components of biotechnological projects are manpower expertise and appropriate resources. At present in India, there are not many organizations, that can independently take up a project from inception to the market. Hence, DBT and BCIL are jointly working on these vital issues. With the creation of BCIL and the new liberalized policies of the Government of India, several companies have set up modern facilities for large-scale production of antibiotics like penicillin, tetracycline, and streptomycin etc. A plant was put into operation for the production of HFS near Madras. A few companies have launched their products, based on tissue culture. One such big plant was set up in Cochin. Several pharmaceutical firms are marketing immuno-diagnostic kits for the early detection of pregnancy and diseases like amoebiasis, hepatitis and typhoid. Recently, an indigenously developed kit for early detection of pregnancy was launched. Many other diagnostics kits are likely to touch the market soon. The Government of India has approved a number of new industrial licenses/foreign collaborations in the area of agriculture, environmental and food biotechnology, and yet many more are under active consideration. However, there has been a significant increase in Government of India's outlays for biotechnology over the past decade. Since the time of establishment, in 1986, the allocation for the Department has increased manifold. The budgetary allocations have gone up from Rs. 404 million in 1987-88 to Rs. 1,138 million in 1997-98 and by 2001-2002 it became Rs. 1,863 million. Though the current price allocation figures may not give a complete picture but the budgeted figure for 2002-03 shows a doubling of allocation to Rs. 2,356 million. In India the developmental allocations are generally made for five years under the National Five Year Plans. The Government has recently finalized the Tenth Five Year Plan (2002-2007). The Working Group on Science and Technology for the Tenth Five Year Plan, constituted by the Planning Commission, has proposed an outlay of Rs. 20,750 million for the period 2002 to 2007 (Table 4.2). This marks a sharp increase of 234 per cent from the budgetary provisions made during the Ninth Plan period (1997-2002) which totaled at Rs. 6,215 million only. The Vision Statement for the Tenth Five Year Plan enumerates the proposal for human genome sequences, proteomics, structural biology and bioinformatics. The DBT has established a huge infrastructure for bioinformatics. There are almost 55 bioinformatics centres working as a strong information network in the country, linked with databases and networks around the world for easy access by large number of scientists. Similarly, the DBT has supported 51 courses at different academic institutions all over the country to meet the growing demand of skilled manpower in the country as discussed later. The DBT has 17 task forces in different areas of importance each comprising 12-13 experts who help in recommending and monitoring of R&D projects. The DBT has launched an innovative scheme of developing institutional clusters to exploit the institutional and academic synergies and economise on resources. Recently, micro propagation technology parks have been established at the Tata Energy Research Institute, New Delhi and the National Chemical Laboratory, Pune. They are serving as an important interface not only between the industry and the developers of technology in the areas of plant tissue culture but also among the academic institutions. Technologies for Eucalyptus, Teak and Bamboo have been transferred to Cadila Pharmaceuticals Limited. On the similar lines three turnkey projects have been developed by these centres for three different federal states in collaboration with respective academic institutions.

The DBT has taken special precaution to find crucial balance between different sections of society as far as technology absorption is concerned apart from promoting industrial Development. It is supporting low-cost biotechnology adoption programmes for socially backward communities. The programmes include vermi-composting, use of organic manure, silkworm rearing, mushroom cultivation, etc. Some training cum demonstration programmes are also being supported for them. Efforts are also on for gender mainstreaming. The DBT has launched 11 projects for women in the areas of waste management, bio pesticides, biofertilizers, floriculture, fish farming for poor women in the rural areas. At the Golden Jubilee Biotechnology Park for Women, industrial modules have been allotted to women entrepreneurs for setting up units in the above-mentioned areas. This park was inaugurated in 1998 near Chennai the capital of a southern Indian state Tamil Nadu. The park is located in Siruseri, adjacent to Information Technology Park in an area of about 20 acres. It would have some central facilities for the entrepreneurs for technology resourcing, training and marketing. This is a first unique project of a joint effort by the central and state government in the realm of biotechnology.

In recent times, DBT has taken up a proactive role in promotion of industry. DBT proposed a single window application-processing cell as part of a new regulatory system for the domestic biotechnology sector. The move formed part of the recent recommendations on biotechnology sector made by the Confederation of Indian Industry (CII). Besides recommending setting up of a single window application-processing cell at DBT, CII had also suggested a fixed time frame of 150 days for clearing new biotech proposals. In this regard, CII had recommended a process whereby a new application would be sent by the single window agency to the Review Committee on Genetic Manipulation (RCGM), which in turn would be required to submit a scientific evaluation report within 60 days of receiving the applications. This report will be submitted to the relevant approval committee, identified by the end product category. For example, in case of agricultural products, it would go to the Genetic Engineering

Approval Committee (GEAC), in case of pharmaceutical products to the Drugs and Pharma Approval Committee (DPAC), and in case of food products to the Biotech Foods Approval Committee (BFAC). The GEAC/DPAC/BFAC would be required to accord approval or rejection within 90 days of receiving the evaluation report from RCGM. In case of rejection of the application, the applicants will also have the right to appeal to the concerned approval committee. CII had also suggested that any additional information required by RCGM for completeness of the application form would have to be called for within 30 days of receipt of the application. Besides DBT, the recommendations were submitted by CII to 14 other agencies, including seven ministries. Most of the recommendations submitted by CII have been accepted by DBT. It can be seen from Table 4.2 that the examples of some important technologies developed through DBT supported by Indian Institutions and transferred to local industries. Also it can be seen that the approved rDNA products in Indian Market and Major biotechnology companies involved in the area of recombinant biopharmaceuticals through Tables 4.3 and 4.4.

Technology Transfer

The early initiatives of transfer of biotechnology research leads, protocols and technologies to industry, have been spearheaded by Govt., Science and Technology (S&T) Organizations particularly the DBT. Biotechnology Consortium India Ltd., was established in 1990 to act as an agency for forging linkages between research, financial and industrial institutions and the Government agencies. There are successes stories in which the development transfer of indigenous technologies through public funded institutions. Some of the examples and significant developments in the areas of modern biotechnology, which have been introducing in the market are very clearly shown in Table 4.2 and 4.3. Also, the major biotech companies involved in the area of rDNA are listed in Table 4.4.

Table 4.2: Technologies developed through DBT

Technology	*Developed by*	*Transferred*
Leprosy immuno-modulator	NII, New Delhi	Cadila Pharmaceuticals Ltd.
Leishmaniasis detection kit	CDRI, Lucknow	Span Diagnostics Ltd.
Western Blot kit for HIV I and II detection	CRI, Mumbai	J.Mitra and Company
Naked eye agglutination system for HIV I and II detection in whole blood	UDSC, New Delhi	Cadila Pharmaceuticals Ltd
Hepatitis C Diagnostics (ELISA) based	ICGEB, New Delhi	X-Cyton, Bangalore
The IgM Mac ELISA kit for the detection of Dengue	NIV, Pune	Zydus Cadila, Ahmedabad
The IgM Mac ELISA kit for the detection of Japanese Encephalitis	NIV, Pune	Zydus Cadila, Ahmedabad
The IgM Mac ELISA kit for the detection of West Nile	NIV, Pune	Zydus Cadila, Ahmedabad
ELISA system to measure alpha-feto-protein (AFP) levels in pregnant women	NIV, Pune	Shanta Biotechnics, Hyderabad
An IgM based system for the detection of Hepatitis A virus using monoclonal/polyclonal antibodies	NIV, Pune	Bharat Biotech, Hyderabad
Urine based systems (ELISA) for the detection of Reproduction Hormones i.e., Pregnodiol Glucurinide (PDG), Esterone Glucuronide (EIG), Follicle Stimulating Hormone (FSH) and Leuteinizing Hormone (LH)	IRR, Mumbai	Zydus Cadila, Ahmedabad
A technology utilizing Yarrowia Lipolytica expressing Hepatitis B surface and pre-S genes	University of Baroda, Baroda	Biological Evans Ltd., Hyderabd.
A technology for expressing HCG using Pichia Pastoris System	IISc, Bangalore	Cadila Pharamaceuticals Ltd.
Recombinant candidate anthrax vaccine	JNU and CBT, Delhi	Panacea Viotec, Delhi

Source: www.dbtindia.org.

Table 4.3: Approved rDNA products in Indian Market

Human Insulin (rHu In)
Erythropoietin (rEPO)
Recombinant hepatitis B vaccine (rHepB Vac)
Human Growth Hormone (rHGH)
Human Interleukin 2 (rhlL2)
Human Interleukin 11 (rhlL11)
Granulocyte Colony Stimulating Factor (rGCSF)
Granulocyte Macrophage Colony Stimulating Factor (rGMCSF)
Interferon a-2a (rinf a-2a)
Interferon a-2b (rinf a-2b)
Interferon Gamma (rinf y)
Blood Factor VIII
Follicle Stimulating Hormone (roFSH)
Tissue Plasminogen Activator (rTPA)
Streptokinase (rSK)
rDrotrecogin-a

Table 4.4: Major biotechnology companies involved in the area of recombinant biopharmaceuticals

Name of the Company	*Products*	*Nature of work*
Aktiva Biotech Ltd., Hyderabad	r-DNA biopharmaceuticals	Research
Bharat Biotech International Ltd, Hyderabad	r-Hepatitis B vaccine, Lysostaphin, streptokinase	Research, manufacturing, marketing
Bhat Biotech Ltd., Bangalore	r-DNA biopharmaceuticals	Research
Biocon India Ltd., Bangalore	Insulin, streptokinase, interferon, human GCSF, erythropoietin	Research, import and marketing
Biological E Ltd, Hyderabad	r-Hepatitis B vaccine	Research, in the process of initiating manufacture
Cadila Healthcare Ltd, Ahmedabad	r-Hepatitis B vaccine, Interferon alpha 2b	Research, import and marketing
Dabur Research Foundation, Ghaziabad	r-DNA biopharmaceuticals	Research
Dano Chemicals Ltd., Hyderabad	r-DNA biopharmaceuticals	Research

(contd.)

(contd.)

Name of the Company	*Products*	*Nature of work*
Dr.Reddy's Laboratories Ltd., Hyderabad	HIV protein (p24, gp36, gp41), GCSF, interferon alpha 2b, r-Hepatitis B vaccine	Research, manufacturing, marketing
East India Pharmaceuticals Ltd., Kolkata	r-DNA biopharmaceuticals	Research
Eli Lilly and Co., Hyderabad	α-Drotrecogin, Insulin, Human Growth Harmone	Import and marketing
Emcure Pharmaceuticals Ltd, Pune	Erythrotoietin, Interleukan, GMCSF	Import and marketing
Full Ford India Ltd, Mumbai	Interferon,	Import and marketing
Glenmark Lab Pvt., Ltd., Mumbai	r-Human Interleukin-2; GCSF and Erythrotoietin	Import and marketing
Indian Immunologicals Hyderabad	r-DNA biopharmaceuticals	Research
Indo Bioactive Labs Pvt. Ltd, Pune	r-DNA biopharmaceuticals	Research
INTAS Pharmaceuticals Ltd, Ahmedabad	Heptatis B Vaccine, GMCSF and Interferon	Import and marketing
Jhonsons and Jhonsons Ltd, Mumabi	Erythrotoietin,	Import and marketing
Kee Pharama, New Delhi	Erythrotoietin, Streptokinase, GCSF	Import and marketing
LG Chemicals, New Delhi	Human growth harmone, Erythrotoietin, Interferon and Insulin	Import and marketing
Lupin Ltd, Mumbai	Interferon alpha 2b	Import and marketing
Medgene Biotech Pvt, Ltd., Hyderabad	r-DNA Pharmacenticals	Research
Novo Nordisc, Mumbai	Human Insulin	Import and marketing
Organon India Ltd, Kolkata	Human follicile stimulating factor	Import and marketing
Panacea Biotech. Ltd. New Delhi	Hepatitits B Vaccine, anthrax vaccing	Research, manufacture, marketing

(contd.)

(contd.)

Name of the Company	*Products*	*Nature of work*
Ranbaxy, New Delhi	Human Erythoro-poietin, GMCSF, Interferon α-2b, hepatitis B Vaccine	Import and marketing
Serum Institute of India Ltd., Pune	FSH, Hepatitis-B	Manufacture, import and marketing
Shantha Biotechnics Pvt. Ltd., Hyderabad	Hepatitis B Vaccine, interferon alpha, streptokinase	Research, manufactuing, marketing
Shasun Chemicals and Drugs Ltd., Chennai	r-DNA Pharmaceuticals	Research
Shreya Life Sciences Ltd., Mumbai	Insulin, r-human growth hormone	Import and marketing
Smith Kline Beeceham	Hepatitis B vaccine combination with DPT; Hepatitis A/B combination vaccine	Import and marketing
SUN pharmaceutical Industries Ltd., Baroda	r-DNA Pharmaceuticals	Research
Torrent Limited, Ahmedabad	Insulin	Research, import
Transgene Biotek Ltd., Hyderabad	r-DNA Pharmaceuticals	Research
USV Ltd., Mumbai	Erythropoietin, human growth hormone, platelet derived growth factor, nerve growth factor	Research
V.H. Bhagat and Co. Ltd., Mumbai	Hepatitis B Vaccine, r-human growth hormone, erythropoietin	Import and marketing
Virchow Biotech Pvt., Ltd., Hyderabad	r-DNA Biopharmaceuticals	Research, setting up manufacturing facility for biopharmaceuticals
Wyeth Lederle, Mumbai	Interleukin-2 and human tumour necrosis factor	Import and marketing
Worckhardt Limited, Aurangabad	Hepatitis B, Insulin Erythropoietin	Research, manufacture, marketing

(contd.)

(contd.)

Name of the Company	*Products*	*Nature of work*
Zydus Cadila Pharmaceuticals Ltd., Ahmedabad	r-erythropoietin, r-hepatitis B Vaccine	Research, import and marketing
Ajeet seeds Co Ltd., Aurangabad	Transgenic cotton	Research, limited field trials
Ankur Seeds Pvt. Ltd., Nagpur	**Transgenic cotton**	Research, limited field trials
Avestha Gengraine Technologies Pvt. Ltd, Bangalore	Transgenic crops	Research
De-Nocil Crop Protection Pvt. Ltd., Mumbai	Transgenic crops	Research
Gaganmal Sugar Industries Ltd., Aurangabad, Maharashtra	Transgenic crops	Research
Hybrid Rice International Ltd., Hyderabad	Transgenic crops	Research, limited field trials
Indo-American Hybrid Seeds (India) Pvt. Ltd., Bangalore	Transgenic tomato	Research, limited field trials
J.K. Seeds Ltd., Secunderabad	Transgenic pigeonpea	Research, limited field trials
Krishdhan Seeds Ltd., Jalana	Bt cotton	Research, limited field trials
Maharashtra Hybrid Seeds Co. Ltd., Mumbai	Bt cotton, transgenic vegetables, corn and rice	Research, and production of Bt cotton
Maharashtra State Seeds Corporation Ltd., Akola	Transgenic cotton	Transgenic crops
Mahendra Hybrid Seeds Co. Ltd., Hyderabad	Transgenic cotton	Research, limited field trials
Metalhelix Life Sciences Private Ltd., Bangalore	Transgenic cotton, Vegetables	Transgenic crops
Monsanto India Pvt. Ltd., Bangalore	Transgenic cotton, Corn	Research, limited field trials

(contd.)

(contd.)

Name of the Company	*Products*	*Nature of work*
Nandi Seeds Co. Pvt. Ltd., Hyderabad, AP	Transgenic crops	Research
Nath Seed Company Ltd., Aurangabad	Transgenic cotton	Research, limited field trials
Nuziveedu Seeds Ltd, Hyderabad	Transgenic cotton	Research
Proagro Seed Company Ltd., Gurgaon	Brassica, mustard, tomato, brinjal, cauliflower, cabbage	Research, limited field trials
Rasi Seeds (P) Ltd., Attur	Transgenic cotton	Research, limited and large scale field trials
SPIC Ltd., Chennai	Transgenic crops	Transgenic crops
Syngenta India Ltd., Aurangabad	Transgenic cotton, maize	Research, limited field trials
Tulasi Seeds Pvt. Ltd., Hyderabad	Transgenic crops	Research, limited field trials

As on January 2004, about 250 institutions, including both from the public and private sector, are involved in activities such as research, import, manufacture or marketing of modern biotech products. Table 4.4 given the names of companies involved with the development and/or commercialization of recombinant therapeutics and transgenic crops, respectively, along with the nature of activities and the products.

Council of Scientific and Industrial Research (CSIR)

The Council of Scientific and Industrial Research was established in 1942. It is India's largest research and development organization. It has 40 laboratories and 80 field stations/extension centres spread over the length and breadth of the country. The total allocation for CSIR in the year 2000-01 was Rs. 9120 million, which is 13 per cent higher from 1999-2000 (Rs. 7940 million). CSIR's Centre for Cellular and Molecular Biology (CCMB) incubated India's first recombinant protein product from a private company, Shantha Biotech, a hepatitis B vaccine and it has numerous industrial relationships, including a joint venture with Biological E and Amersham

Pharmacia to build DNA micro-arrays. CSIR proposes to continue programmes in the area of agro-biotechnology, industrial biotechnology, and toxicant identification control, with a strategy for controlled change in direction as dictated by market needs. Strategic alliances would thus be sought for programmes for understanding the processes, molecular genetics and control of gene expression, genetic manipulation of microbes, recombinant DNA products, engineering new protein molecules/new chemical entities, development of immuno-diagnostics and biotechnology of prospective medicinal and aromatic plants.

Indian Council of Medical Research (ICMR)

Another major institution working in the area of biotechnology is the Indian Council for Medical Research (ICMR) under the Ministry of Health. It is the apex body in the country to promote, coordinate and formulate biomedical and health research. Central Government gives full maintenance grant to the council, to research in communicable diseases, contraception, maternity and child health, nutrition, non-communicable and basic research. The total allocation for ICMR from the Central Government (Ministry of Health) was Rs. 1470 million in 2000-01, which was 21 per cent higher over the previous year allocation, that is 1999-2000 (Rs. 1160 million). The Council is also engaged in research on tribal health, traditional medicine and publication and dissemination of information. In the year 2001 ICMR has launched a major programme in the field of genomics (vector, microbial, human) with the initial allocation of Rs. 510 million. One of the major areas of focus is the disease susceptibility gene identification, especially for, communicable diseases like leprosy, tuberculosis, non-communicable diseases as rheumatic fever or genetic diseases as thalissimia. ICMR has established four centres for developing molecular medicine at All India Institute of Medical Sciences (AIIMS), New Delhi, Sanjay Gandhi Post Graduate Institute of Medical Sciences (SGPGIMS), Lucknow, Jawaharlal Nehru University (JNU), New Delhi and Post Graduate

Institute of Medical Education and Research (PGIMER), Chandigarh. Apart from this, ICMR has also established six biomedical informatics units in different parts of the country. It has proposed an allocation of Rs. 1000 million for the Tenth Five Year Plan. (See Table 4.6)

Indian Council for Agriculture Research (ICAR)

In India, agricultural research is being spearheaded by the Indian Council of Agricultural Research (ICAR) under the Ministry of Agriculture. The Council is engaged in conducting research in the field of agriculture, soil and water conservation, animal husbandry, fisheries, dairying, forestry and also agricultural education. The allocation for ICAR from the Ministry of Agriculture was Rs. 13,990 million in 2000-01, which was Rs. 12,060 million in the previous year. It has several research laboratories all over the country conducting research in biotechnology, besides using traditional breeding techniques for different research projects. ICAR has established a National Research Centre on Plant Biotechnology (NRCPB) at the Indian Agricultural Research Institute (IARI), Pusa, New Delhi, which is fully dedicated to work on plant biotechnology. Annual expenditure over the projects at NRCPB is Rs. 150 million. Besides, ICAR has also supported two research networks, combining ICAR and even non-ICAR research laboratories to work on crops like rice, cotton, brasica and brinzal. ICAR is also implementing a World Bank supported programme called National Agriculture Technology Programme (NATP) through which huge allocations have been made at different research laboratories for strengthening infrastructure for biotechnological research. ICAR has also collaborated with DBT and Rockfeller Foundation to jointly launch a National Rice Biotechnology Network (NRBN) in 1988. This project helped in evolving a culture of collaboration among different institutions, which has led to publication of several international papers in established journals. This network put together plant breeders and molecular biologists on the one hand and also provoked interests of private sector in R&D.

For instance, Mahyco and Rockfeller Foundation worked together on identifying the relevant genes for saving Indian rice from brown plant hoppers. In this collaborative effort, interaction was not limited to private entities only. It is between private and public sector organizations also. Several universities also have tie ups with private sector organisations. For instance, Tamil Nadu Agricultural University (TNAU) attempted joint trials with Monsanto on weed resistance in soil. TNAU was also partner in monitoring the Bt Cotton field trials of Mahyco-Monsanto alliance. TNAU is also holding in exploratory talks with Rasi seeds (it is also in alliance with Monsanto) to conduct and monitor field trials of Bt crops. Similarly, rice research work at National Research Centre for Plant Biotechnology has attracted business interest of companies like Nath Seeds Ltd. and JK Agri-genetics.

Human Resource Development (HRD)

The National Biotechnology Board had launched an integrated short-term training programme way back in 1984, to cope up with growing demand for highly trained manpower. In the first phase (1984-85), 5 universities were selected for initiating M.Sc./M.Tech programme in this multi-disciplinary area. Subsequently, in 1985-86 and 1986-87, the DBT has added 8 universities/institutions for M.Sc/M.Tech/Post-doctoral teaching programmes. Subsequently, DBT was entrusted with the responsibility of evolving curriculum for biotechnology courses and meet the demand for human resources in the field of biotechnology. In 1986-87 a model system of post-graduate/post-doctoral teaching in biotechnology in 7 universities/institutions was launched. Some of the specialised M.Sc. courses in marine and agricultural biotechnology were launched in 1988-89 at 3 universities. In 1992-93, DBT supported a five year Integrated Programme in biochemical engineering and biotechnology in Indian Institute of Technology, Delhi and a post-doctoral programme at Indian Agricultural Research Institute, New Delhi.

Now, DBT is supporting 20 M.Sc. courses in general biotechnology, 4 in agricultural biotechnology, one each in medical and marine biotechnology while couple of diploma courses in molecular and biochemical technology. The total intake of students in the various postgraduate courses supported by the DBT in the country is around 550 per year. As a part of restructuring of the post doctoral research and training programme, DBT has scraped the on going programme with different institutions and has given this responsibility to Indian Institute of Science (IISc), Bangalore. This is to ensure competitive attitude and quality output in the life sciences. It is being proposed that IISc would award up to 75 fellowships of two-year duration in different streams of biotechnology. DBT is also supporting overseas associateship and short-term training courses for at least 22-25 scientists in a particular year for exposing Indian scientists to newer trends in R&D. This helps working researchers and scientists to upgrade their knowledge and research areas of interest. In this context, services of Biotech Consortium India Limited (BCIL), New Delhi, a DBT floated organisation, are also being used to bridge the scientific knowledge of DBT supported associates and industry requirement. The State Governments are also exploring various options to finance higher education in such advanced technologies. Recently Karnataka government has established an Institute of Bioinformatics and Applied Biotechnology (IBAB), in collaboration with ICICI Ventures to offer a postgraduate course in bioinformatics on its International Technology Park campus. As part of a wider effort for capacity building in institutes of higher learning, full-fledged departments of biotechnology are being set up. The Indian Institute of Science, Bangalore, Indian Institute of Information Technology and Management, Gwalior; and select Regional Engineering Colleges are setting up departments of biotechnology. The All India Council for Technical Education (AICTE) has already approved B.Tech. programmes in biotechnology in eight engineering colleges and has advised to develop a model curriculum for undergraduate programmes. All the new departments will have undergraduate, post-graduate and doctoral programmes. Special funding will be provided for the purpose in the Tenth Five Year Plan. Apart from expanding teaching of biotechnology at higher educational institutions a separate module on biotechnology would also be integrated with the school curriculum. The Department of Biotechnology of Government of India will provide the necessary outline of this module so that the National Council of Education Research and Training (NCERT) and the Boards of School Education would be accordingly advised.

University Grants Commission of India has come out with a scheme to promote higher centres of learning at one place and assist them as much as possible. In this regard, Delhi based Jawaharlal Nehru University (JNU) has been identified by the UGC as centre for excellence in the areas of genomics, genetics and biotechnology. The University has received funds of Rs. 300 million and is planning to start a new integrated M.Sc./ Ph.D programme in life sciences and biotechnology and is setting up a modern animal house for experiments. Efforts are also being made to up grade equipment and library facilities. The new integrated programme in life sciences will reduce the time taken by a scholar to complete his Ph.D by at least within two years. Now the scholar 95 not required to undergo a separate M.Phil programme. JNU is aiming at 10 seats for the integrated course and another 20-25 seats in the School of Life Sciences. The University has so far received 40 proposals for possible projects, which can be pursued by them in these fields in the future. Out of the funds that JNU has finally managed to get from the UGC on its selection as the University with potential for excellence, Rs. 100 million have been set aside for upgradation of facilities and equipments. The rest of the Rs. 200 million would help University to subscribe to some of the 8,000 online journals, both in the filed of science and social sciences. Besides this, JNU also announced recruitment of more researchers. The tie-ups with industry are also likely to grow. For instance, researchers at the Centre for Biotechnology (CBT) at Jawaharlal Nehru University in New Delhi have been working for four years on a recombinant anthrax vaccine and soon would start Phase I clinical trials in collaboration with Panacea Biotech Ltd. (New Delhi). Hence, there are almost

30 universities offering M.Sc in Biotechnology through a joint entrance examination being conducted by the JNU. Apart from this Goa University is offering a two years Master of Science course in Marine Biotechnology, while All India Institute of Medical Sciences (AIIMS) offers a similar course in medical biotechnology. There are a couple of institutions offering Post Graduate Diploma Courses in molecular and biochemical technology as well as Bioinformatics. Indian Institute of Technology (IIT) at New Delhi and Kharagpur offer a Five Year integrated course in biochemical engineering and biotechnology. There is a Post MD/MS Certificate Course in medical biotechnology being offered by Post Graduate Institute of Medical Education and Research, Chandigarh and Sanjay Gandhi Post Graduate Institute of Medical Education and Research, Lucknow. Thus the role of government in financing biotechnology research in India is very significant through budgetary allocations under Five Year Plans see Table 4.5 and 4.6.

Table 4.5: Budgetary Allocations of Major Funding Agencies in India

(Rs. Million)

	1990-91	*2000-01*	% *Change*
Department of Scientific and Industrial Research (DSIR)	131.3	583.8	344.63
Department of Science and Technology (DST)	2588.9	7798	201.20
Department of Biotechnology (DBT)	655	1361	107.78
Indian Council of Agriculture Research (ICAR)	3236	13990	332.32
Indian Council of Medical Research (ICMR)	396	1470	271.21
Council of Scientific and Industrial Research (CSIR)	2351	9120	287.92
University Grants Commission (UGC)	3495	14070	302.57

Source: RIS based on budgetary papers of relevant years, Ministry of Finance, Government of India.

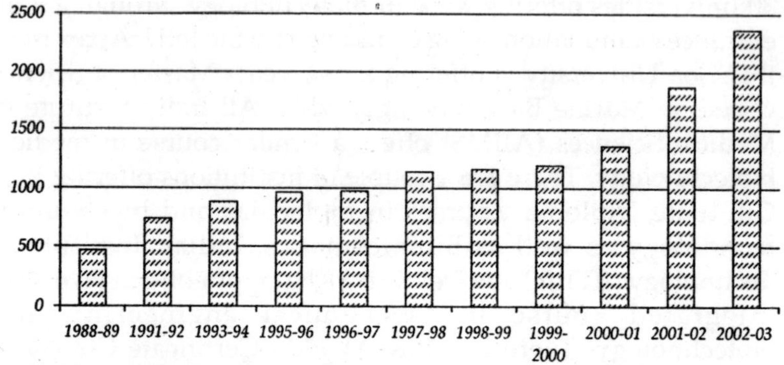

Figure 4.1: Budgetary Allocations to Department of Biotechnology

Table 4.6: Allocations for Biotechnology under Five Year Plans

(Rs. In Million)

Sl. No.	*Name of the Scheme*	*Ninth Plan*	*Tenth Plan*
01	Biotech Facilities, Centres of Excellence and Programme Support	680.46 (10.95)	900.00 (4.34)
02	Research and Development		
	2.1 Agriculture Biotechnology	1651.26 (26.56)	550.00 (2.65)
	2.2 Medical Biotechnology	808.88 (13.01)	4130.00 (31.46)
	2.3 Environmental Biotechnology	128.72 (2.07)	200.00 (0.96)
	Total	**2588.86 (41.65)**	**7280.00 (35.08)**
03	Biotechnology for Societal Development	—	250.00 (1.20)
04	Bio-Process and Product Development		
	4.1 Food Biotechnology	—	250.00 (1.20)
	4.2 Microbial and Industrial Biotechnology	—	250.00 (1.20)
	4.3 IPR and Biosafety	7.51 (0.12)	100.00 (0.48)
	4.4 Programmes Merged with other heads	513.05 (8.25)	—
	Total	**520.55 (8.38)**	**600.00 (2.89)**

(Contd.)

(Contd.)

Sl. No.	*Name of the Scheme*	*Ninth Plan*	*Tenth Plan*
05	International Cooperation	109.37 (1.76)	400.00 (1.93)
06	Human Resource Development	1000.00 (16.09)	160.00 (0.77)
07	Bioinformatics	700.00 (11.26)	120.00 (0.58)
08	Autonomous Institutes		
	08.1 National Institute of Immunology	642.74 (10.34)	2080.00 (10.02)
	08.2 National Care for Cell Science	343.86 (5.53)	800.00 (3.86)
	08.3 Centre for DNA Finger Printing and Diagnostics	313.62 (5.05)	1130.00 (5.45)
	08.4 National Brain Research Centre	130.00 (2.09)	700.00 (4.92)
	08.5 National Centre for Plan Genome Research	101.00 (1.62)	700.00 (3.37)
	08.6 Institute of Bioresources and Sustainable Development	—	170.00 (0.82)
09	I & M Sector	—	3620.00 (17.45)
	Secretariate	100.00 (1.61)	10.00 (0.05)
	Grand Total	**6215.42 (100.00)**	**20750.00 (100.00)**

Note: Figures in parentheses are share in total.
Source: RIS Based on DBT Reports.

Initiatives by State Governments

In recent past several State Governments in India have taken initiatives to attract biotechnology industry to their respective States. Tamil Nadu has announced its biotechnology policy in September 2000, while Karnataka followed the same in February 2001. In the same year Andhra Pradesh was seeking to leverage its strengths in the pharmaceuticals, agriculture and IT services to put it at the forefront of the biotechnology race among the various State Governments. Not surprisingly, the

States have extended similar concessions, already available to the IT sector.

Andhra Pradesh (AP)

As part of the AP-BT policy, among other things, the companies would enjoy a lower sales tax of just one per cent, down from the present 8 to 16 per cent, on all high-end biotechnology products produced within the State. They would also be able to book space at concessional rates at the proposed 600 square kilometre Genome Valley. The policy proposes setting up an exclusive Rs. 500 million venture capital fund. The policy also speaks of funding the biotechnology start-ups through the existing APIDC Venture Capital Ltd (APIDC-VCL). The aim of the policy is to leverage on the existing strengths of the state for rapid commercialization of biotechnology so that innovative biotechnology products and services could be produced in the State. AP has already numerous centres of excellence in healthcare, agriculture, and biotechnology. Its capital Hyderabad has earned an image of being the pharmaceutical and science capital of the country. The government is also trying to use its strength in the IT for the growth of bioinformatics in the State. For the rapid growth of this sector, the government has identified field diagnostics, therapeutics, pharmacogenomics, bioinformatics, agriculture, marine, industrial biotechnology and contract research as some of the thrust areas. ICICI has established a Knowledge Park at Turkapally near Hyderabad, for promotion of life sciences by investing Rs. 310 million on a 200-acre site which is a joint initiative of ICICI and the Andhra Pradesh Government. The ICICI Knowledge Park and the Biotechnology Park together form part of a larger blueprint of the Genome Valley project, which the Government plans to develop on a 600 sq. km area encompassing Medchal, Shameerpet, Kesara mandals in Rangareddi district and Uppal-Tarnaka ICICI has signed an MOU with the Indian Institute of Chemical Technology (IICT), Centre for Cellular and Molecular Biology (CCMB) and the University of Hyderabad, in a new 'knowledge network initiative'. This project has also been assisted by the Department of Scientific and Industrial Research (DSIR), to the tune of Rs. 15 million to set up a Virtual Information Project taken up by the Knowledge Park. The Park has been licensed under Section 25 of the Companies Department of Scientific and Industrial Research, Government of India for the benefit of customs duty exemption and Excise duty waiver. Under the initiative, 26 partners in the Knowledge Park will get on-line access to library-based information expertise from these national labs and university system. It would also encourage undertaking collaborative research between corporates and research companies based in the park. The park has identified another 20 premier research organizations and universities during the first phase of the programme. At this point, only two start-ups-Medicorp Technologies and Pulsar Electro-Optics Ltd, have moved into the park with their projects. Two more companies are actively considering to move in. They are Bijam Biosciences Ltd, a Nagarjuna Group company which wants to set up a research centre in agri-biotech and MedGene Biotech, which plans to start a research centre for new drug discovery and genomics research. Interestingly, one of the beneficiaries of the Knowledge Park is the proposed Rs. 900 million Biotechnology Park coming up within the vicinity. The Biotechnology Park, to be developed on a 150-acre site, has been initiated as a joint venture of the Andhra Pradesh Government and Shapoorji Pallonji, a Mumbai based construction company. In the MoU the state government would be a minority stakeholder. The private promoter would be responsible for designing, construction, financing, marketing and maintaining the park. During the first phase, the park would focus on therapeutics, diagnostics and industrial biotechnology. Revenues would primarily come through leasing of premises, equipment and rental for operations. Meanwhile, the company has applied for a Central Government grant of Rs. 150 million. The Department of Biotechnology, Government of India has rolled out a programme for biotechnology parks in various states, under which grants would be sanctioned depending upon the nature of the business plans.

Karnataka

The Karnataka Government has announced a biotechnology policy to promote this sector and is setting up an institute for bioinformatics in Bangalore. The Government is also creating a biotechnology fund which will have inflows from biotechnology companies. This would be used for incubation of new projects and promotion of the sector in the State. The policy statement spells this out as an attempt to tap on the synergy between information technology and biotechnology as IT can immensely help in biotechnology research to achieve results faster. The Karnataka Government is putting in Rs. 50 million and an equal amount is being brought in by ICICI to develop the Institute of Bioinformatics and Applied Biotechnology in Bangalore. The renowned biotechnology expert, Dr. H. Sharat Chandra will look after the institute as Chairman. The institute will have four primary objectives:

(1) Conducting research in biotechnology,
(2) Providing education and training in similar areas;
(3) Providing incubation facilities for start-up projects with common facilities; and
(4) Creating a platform for educationist, scientists, industry, venture funds and Government, to interact with each other for the development of the sector in India.

Karnataka has planned to launch India's first state-sponsored biotechnology venture capital fund to boost their initiatives. The fund is likely to have an initial seed capital of Rs. 100 million to be operated through Karnataka State Industrial Investment and Development Corporation (KSIIDC)-Karnataka State Finance Corporation (KSFC). Karnataka was also the frontrunner in setting up the first state financed IT VC fund. It now proposes to extend Bangalore's number one position in IT to other knowledge-based industries by floating a fund to support subjects like biotechnology, genetic engineering and pharmaceuticals. To supplement the modest initial contribution, the state has plans to mobilize additional funds for the biotechnology corpus from other domestic and global Financial Institutions and multilateral agencies. Recently, Karnataka's IT and commerce-industries team tried to pitch for a share in the $ 1.2 billion incubation fund of Singapore's National Science and Technology Board (NSTB).

The Karnataka officials scoured for opportunities for financial, technical and marketing assistance for biotechnology ventures, besides aiming for joint R&D between Institute of Bioinformatics in Bangalore and Centre for Cellular and Molecular Biology, Hyderabad, and two top Singapore agencies namely Institute of Molecular and Cellular Biology (IMCB) and Institute of Agribiology (IAB). Incidentally, as part of the biotechnology buildup. The Karnataka government is also setting up an ultra-modern Centre for Human Genetics at the Agriculture University campus in Bangalore over a 20-acre plot. It has also engaged Arthur Andersen to prepare a biotechnology strategy paper spelling out the infrastructure and policy framework required to boost its growth and to extract optimum advantage from this stream of new business.

Tamil Nadu (TN)

The Tamil Nadu Industrial Development Corporation (TIDCO) has linked a technical service agreement with Cornell University, USA for setting up a biotechnology park in Chennai, christened TICEL (Tidco Centre for Life Sciences), the park proposes to attract fresh investment of Rs. 10,000 million from 50 new companies to be set up in the park and fuel bioentrepreneurship. Among the states, Tamil Nadu is the only state, with such kind of foreign 28 collaboration. This initiatives will put Chennai on the global network of Cornell, which has technical collaboration in 36 countries. TICEL is modelled on the TIDEL Park, the information technology park set up by TIDCO. As per the MoU, valid for five years renewable for another five years, Cornell University will help from the conceptual stage to the commissioning stage of the park. The state-of-the-art park will provide complete technical and other allied services under one umbrella including technology transfer, monitoring, networking, contract and collaborative research work, product validation, documentation, commercialization, training and a separate intellectual property rights (IPR) cell which will support in the areas of patents, licencing, royalty sharing and copyrights. The total cost is pegged at Rs. 625 million. TIDCO will be investing Rs. 90 million as equity. The Tamil Nadu government would bring in Rs. 200 million, while the remaining Rs. 330 million would be raised from various banks and financial institutions. It is stated that State Bank of India, Industrial Development Finance Corporation and Exim Bank have also shown interest in picking up equity state. The financial closure of the park is over in November 2001, and the park was made ready for occupation by December 2002. Cornell University in addition to the above, will also be setting up a special project cell at its premises in the USA to provide for advanced training, apart from offering access to its electronic library. It will also facilitate relationships between the tenants of similar parks abroad and in the Chennai park besides exchange of faculty for conducting specific and advanced training programmes. TICEL would be set up in a five acre expense consisting of two major facilities—a bio-resource center of 18,000 sq. ft. and customized laboratories of 1.2 lakh sq. ft. It will explore the Indian genetic pool and exploit the germplasm base available and leverage on the existing pool of Indian biotechnology scientists and low cost software skills.

Himachal Pradesh (HP)

Himachal Pradesh probably is the only Northern Indian state which has prepared a blue print for promotion of biotechnology industries in the State. This would include setting up of a biotechnology park at Solan, conservation and exploitation of bioresearches, intensification of R&D, and promoting biotechnology entrepreneurship through tax concessions and relaxed labour laws. At Solan, land has been earmarked at New Solan to set up the biotech industries. The idea is to tap the huge potential of bio-resources and commercially exploit the state's rare herbal medicines, annual global trade flow of which is close to $20 billion. It is also proposed to provide research based support to the private companies in form of providing for instance, access to a database of bio resources which is being developed along with separate entries of endangered medicinal plants. Apart from this a germ plasm collection and culture facilities and bioinformatics network is also being established. In order to tap these strengths, a series of concessions and sops have been chalked out. The industry has been given priority sector status and assured uninterrupted power supply at industrial rates. Labour laws have been relaxed, arrangements made for single window clearance of projects, with mega project status for ones with over Rs. 500 million investment. This would encourage diversification of farming through companies which are already into micro propagation units in other states for plants and crops like ginger, saffron, potato, strawberry and bamboo.

5

Venture Capital Financing of Biotechnology

Investments in Indian biotechnology have begun with the early initiatives of government and setting up of separate department of biotechnology. Five-year plans are made for such investment by the department for promoting biotechnology R&D, human resource development, establishment of biotech facilities, product and processes development and other activities. Besides DBT, other Government S&T agencies such as Indian Council for Agricultural Research (ICAR), Council of Scientific and Industrial Research (CSIR), Indian Council of Medical Research (ICMR), University Grants Commission (UGC) and Department of Science and Technology (DST) also support R&D programs in biotechnology. On the other hand private sector investment has also been picking up since 1997 and particularly visible after the announcement of draft human genome sequence in the year 2000. However, such investments are not sufficient to the sector to boost up itself as BT is characterized by intensive research efforts, long gestation period, high costs and promotional investment for development, highly risk oriented and take significant time to come out as an out put from the research in laboratory, as well as probable in nature in its result and stringent regulation compared to IT. So, the biotechnology companies/projects whether they are small, medium or big would require larger amount of investment for their success and commercialization, particularly for start-up companies with scientists', technocrats together with small investors as promoters. Hence, the traditional investors like bankers, financial institutions and others may not come forward to promote such projects of biotechnology development as they look for higher returns at lower degree of risk. Then a question arises here that who can finance such type of projects when traditional financers are not ready to put their money? The solution for these new, innovative and promising technological projects is venture capital.

Venture capital is the capital available for financing new business ventures. It is also often thought of as the early stage financing of new and young enterprises seeking to grow rapidly. In a broad sense the venture capital refers to capital investment made in a business or industrial enterprise that carries high elements of risk, insecurity and probability of business hazards. Capital investment may assume the form of either equity or debt or both i.e. Derivative investments. The risk associates with the enterprise could be so high as to entail total loss or be so insignificant as to lead to high gains. However, venture capital finance is different from conventional finance i.e. money lending and bank finance, because venture capital financier takes keen interest in business performance of the investees' firm. Thus venture capital is the engine that can finance the growth of knowledge based industries worldwide and has become very popular in different parts of country, as it is instrumental for industrial development by exploiting vast and untapped potentialities.

Traditionally, the role of venture capital was an extension of the developmental financial institutions like IDBI, ICICI, SIDBI and State Finance Corporations (SFCs). The first origins of modern Venture Capital in India can be traced to the setting up of a Technology Development Fund (TDF) in the year 1987-88, through the levy of a cess on all technology import payments. TDF was meant to provide financial assistance—to innovative and high-risk technological programs through the Industrial Development Bank of India. This measure was followed up in November 1988, by the issue of guidelines by the (then) Controller of Capital Issues (CCI). These stipulated the framework for the establishment and operation of funds/ companies that could avail of the fiscal benefits extended to them. In fact, the venture capital industry in India has emerged after the Government of India announced guidelines in 1988 for setting up venture capital funds (VCFs). These guidelines restricted the setting up of VCFs by banks or financial institutions only. Later, in September 1995, Government of India, issued guidelines for overseas venture capital investment in India whereas the Central Board of Direct Taxes (CBDT) issued guidelines for tax exemption purposes. As a part of its mandate to regulate and develop the Indian capital markets, Securities and Exchange Board of India (SEBI) framed the SEBI (Venture Capital Funds) Regulations, 1996. While only 8 domestic VCFs were registered with SEBI during 1996-98, more than 30 additional funds have already been registered for 2000-01. In the final Budget of 2000-01, the Finance Minister announced SEBI as the single point nodal agency for registration and regulation of both domestic and overseas venture capital funds. Now, there are almost 70 VCFs with a focus on India. Their cumulative assets under management would be somewhere close to $5 billion. The figures from the Indian Venture Capital Association (IVCA) reveal that, till 2000, around Rs. 22,000 million (US$ 500 million) had been committed by the domestic VCFs and offshore funds which are members of IVCA. The figures available from private sources indicate that overall funds committed are around US$ 1.3 billion. It is being hoped that by 2008, India would have $10 billion invested through VCFs. India witnessed the second highest disbursement of venture capital in the Asia-Pacific region during 2001 at $ 1.1 billion across 91 companies. Japan received the highest disbursement in the region with $1.8 billion being invested in 39 companies. In contrast, China received only $393 million during the year across 11 companies, which placed it in sixth place among the 13 major markets, which constitute the region. While the total disbursement of $1.1 billion in 2001 was marginally lower than the previous year's (2000) $11.3 billion. The situation was changed during the year 2003 with total disbursement of $2 billion (according to the annual strategic review of the Indian IT industry by the National Association of Software and Services Companies (NASSCOM)). The pattern of VC disbursements last year indicates a preference for late-stage funding. According to the findings of the review of NASSCOM' s study, seed funding accounted for only 15 per cent of the total disbursement, while late-stage funding constituted 41 per cent. Deal sizes have also undergone a change. First round funding saw deal sizes in the range of $1-1.5 million, second round deal sizes were in the region of $3-5 million, third round deals ranged between $4-8 million and deals in the fourth round were in the region of $5-15 million. The 70 VCs operating in India have $5.6 billion in assets under management. There has also been a significant shift to non-internet investments, with the share of non-internet investments increasing to 68 per cent in 2001 against 28 per cent in 2000. VCs have moved to longer gestation investments such as health, biotechnology; IT enabled services and wireless applications. Hence, consolidated VC pool in the Asia-Pacific region is estimated at $81.2 billion.

With the increased role of established private sector as well as start up companies investing in biotechnology, several financial institutions/agencies both in public and private sector have launched venture capital funding mechanism. The Ministry of Science and Technology has provided these opportunities through the establishment of Technology Development Board (TDB) in 1992 for providing financial assistance to industrial concerns and other agencies attempting development and commercialization of indigenous technology or adopting imported technology for wider domestic application. The board has been helpful particularly in promoting several new start-up companies. Since its formation the board has signed 100 agreements with commercial enterprises/agencies with a total projects cost of Rs.15 billion and commitments of Rs.3.58 billion financial assistance to areas of health and medicine engineering and electronics, chemicals and lubricants, agriculture and biotechnology, waste utilization etc. Companies such as M/s Shanta Biotech and M/s Bharat Biotech Producing Recombinant Hepatitis Vaccine, M/s ABL biotech in marine biotechnology are some known and successful beneficiaries. Venture Capital Funding (VCF) in India for biotechnology projects picked up with success stories of TDB in the hands of the prominent VC firms, including Industrial Credit and Investment Corporation of India (ICICI), Morgan Stanley and Small Industrial Development Bank of India (SIDBI) are active. Hence the venture capital is mostly available to companies whose product and market are clearly identified and research leads are already available for commercialization. So, eventually it can be said that venture capital is only the way of promoting and developing the biotechnologies for the betterment of the society.

The biotechnology commitments by different VCFs amount to almost Rs. 3000 million. Out of this, Indian Credit and Investment Corporation of India (ICICI) and Small Industries Development Bank of India (SIDBI) have almost similar commitments for biotechnology while new entrants like Kerela Venture Capital Fund (KVCF) has committed Rs. 200 million, which is just 4 per cent of the total venture capital. SIDBI and ICICI have devoted Rs. 1000 million and Rs. 1700 million respectively. The two other southern states pro-actively supporting biotechnology through venture capital are Andhra Pradesh and Karnataka. Andhra Pradesh Industrial Development Corporation (APIDC) has devoted Rs. 500 million, which is 18 per.cent of the total amount available at the national level while Karnataka State Industrial Infrastructure Development Corporation (KSIIDC) share 7 per cent with an allocation of Rs. 100 million. Some of the major biotechnology VCFs in India along with their specific initiatives is being discussed very clearly herewith.

ICICI

ICICI Venture currently manages/11 funds, aggregating about US$ 400, milling it one of the large private equity investors in the country. Consistent with its strategy of focussing on sectors where Indian companies have a global competitive advantage, all of the ICICI Venture funds make investments only in companies belonging to the IT, life sciences and services sectors. These industries have demonstrated a capability to leverage the intellectual capital in India to effectively address the global markets. ICICI Venture is currently in the process of constituting a dedicated incubator fund for funding start-ups in the area of biotechnology and life sciences. As in the area of information technology, the ICICI Venture Incubator team would be extending support services to its incubatee companies, including basic research infrastructure in tie-up with ICICI-Knowledge Park Limited. The targeted fund size is Rs. 1 billion. Recently ICICI Venture Funds and Global Trust Bank have invested $1.5 million in Avestha Gengraine Technologies Pvt. Ltd. (Avesthagen), a fully integrated biotechnology and bioinformatics company based in International Tech Park Ltd (ITPL), Whitefield Avesthagen, operational since August 1999, would be going in for the second round of funding by April 2002 and expect a turnover of Rs. 500 million in five years. The company currently employs 40 workers, out of which 34 are researchers. Focused on genomics and bioinformatics, with expertise in marker-aided selection, genome sequencing, gene discovery, plant transformation, database management, 3D structure-function analysis.

SIDBI

Small Industries Development Bank of India (SIDBI) and Department of biotechnology (DBT) have set up a Rs. 1000 million Biotechnology Development Fund in 1998. This is to encourage private-public partnerships in the small-scale sector as well as to promote entrepreneurship in biotechnology. It is proposed that the DBT would put in Rs. 200 million, while SIDBI would contribute the rest of Rs. 800 million for the fund. Earlier the proposal was of DBT-SIDBI for a Rs. 500 million (Rs. 250 million each) National Biotech Venture Fund but the Planning Commission of India did not agree with that proposal on the pretext that it would be better to leave it to the financial intermediaries (FIs) as it would entail nurturing and monitoring apart from financial management which FIs can do much better. At this stage, finer details of the proposal such as whether to give assistance as soft loans or set in place a programme with an exit clause that would help the fund sustain itself through royalties and so on are being worked out. The proposal is part of a larger industry orientation proposed by the DBT in its Tenth Plan Approach Paper. In collaboration with the Agriculture Ministry, a large number of decentralized production units (at least 1000 for biofertilisers and biopesticides) in the small scale sector are proposed to be established all over the country with new technology packages by the end of the Tenth Plan.

Though venture capitalists were skeptical about biotechnology because of its long gestation period, the situation has changed. Many established pharma firms, and new biotech firms are focusing on biotech health care products. Shanta Biotech placed one million shares to Morgan Stanley and SBI capital Markets in 2000. Banks still remain the major financing source for biotechnology, accounting for 40 percentage of the funding. Where as venture capital accounts for less than 20 per cent of the biotech funding. It is reported that VC investment in biotech in the last one decade has been US$ 100. There has been three sources for venture support, namely off-shore funds, Indian venture funds and Technology Development Board (a Government Public Venture Fund).

Venture Capital Funding (VCF) in India for biotechnology projects picked up with success stories of TDB in the hands of the prominent VC firms, including Industrial Credit and Investment Corporation of India (ICICI), Morgan Stanley and Small Industrial Development Bank of India (SIDBI) are active. Hence the venture capital is mostly available to companies whose product and market are clearly identified and research leads are already available for commercialization.

India is emerging as a biotech hub. Many players have failed to mobilize funds through private placements. The biotechnology industry needs strong venture support. But the VCs feel that they are not getting attractive projects with high growth potential. Universities and research institutes must focus on evolving good project ideas with good business potential. This seems to be an area of weakness of Indian biotechnology industry. A list of VC supported firms and the fund that supported each firm are given in Table 5.1.

Table 5.1: Venture Capital Funded Indian Biotechnology Firms

Company	*Institutions*	*Activity*
Bharat Biotech	TDB. IDBI-VCF. Unlisted	Hepatitis-B. Re combinant make. Valued at over Rs. 200 crores.
Syngene	ICICI-VCF. Unlisted	Indl. Enzymes and CRO
Shantha Biotech	TDB. Unlisted	Hepatitis-B, DNA based vaccine. Last round of investment 700 Crores.
Strand Genomics	UTI-VCG. ICICI-VCF. Unlisted	Bio informatics
Avesthagen	ICICI-VCF. Unlisted	Start up in Agri genetics, contract research
ABL Biotech	TDB. Unlisted	Beta Carotene
Alpa Amins (P) Ltd	TDB. Unlisted	Import substitute drug intermediate anti TB drug
Manukruti Bio-gens (P) Ltd.	TDB. Unlisted	Diagnostics for bacterial endotoxins
Mark Medicines (P) Ltd.	TDB. Unlisted	Bio becton latic acid concentrate
Prathista Industries	TDB. Unlisted	Bio Fertilizers and plant growth
Ajay Biotech (I) Ltd.	TDB. Unlisted	Bio Pesticides
Microplantae	ICICI-VCF. Listed	Tissue Culture
Hindustan Agrigenetics Ltd.	RCTC. Listed	Tissue Culture. Failed due to market conditions
Emergent Genetics	—	Seeds Company
Gum India	ICICI-VCF. Unlisted	
Dodla Dairy Ltd	APIDC-VCF. Unlisted	Milk processing and value added products with technology from IMAC, USA, Good acquisition condition.
Bangalore Genei (P) Ltd	ICICI-VCF.	Restriction enzymes
Vimta Labs	ICICI-VCF. IDBI. listed	Services/Testing Lab moving into biotech services.
Kshema Technologies	GTV	Bio Informatics
X Cyton	SIDBI VCL	Bio Informatics
Gangagen	ICF Ventures	Bio Informatics
Bioserve Biotechnologies Ltd.	APIDC-VCL	Genomic Based Contract Research
Genomik Designs Pharmaceuticals Ltd. (GDPL)	APIDC-VCL	Drug Discovery Research
Silico Insights Biosciences	APIDC-VCL	Genomics Research
Indus Biotechnology Pvt. Ltd	APIDC-VCL	Research on Chronic Disease

Present Status

A comprehensive survey conducted by the Confederation of Indian Industry, CII, indicates that there are currently 160 registered Biotechnology companies in the country. Of these 60 are distinctly engaged in molecular and recombinant biotechnology. More than 50 per cent of these companies are located in Bangalore, and Hyderabad. 75 per cent of these companies have been established in the last 5 years. The total revenues of this sector stand at $150 million in 2002 of which $60 million are exports revenues.

The total Project investment made by the private Biotech companies is estimated at $100 million over the last 5 years. VC funding is small at $15 million which indicates that a large part of the funding has come from other conventional funds. Projected investment over the next 3 years is expected to treble.

As venture capital is found as an ultimate solution for development and promotion of biotechnology, every country has been striving hard to promote it a lot for the purpose of developing the new and innovative technologies to attain the greater heights in agriculture, health and other sectors. So it is very clear that the role of venture capital is very significant in promoting the biotechnology that is an engine for the growth of the economies. Therefore all the countries have realized that the only source for development and promotion of biotechnology is venture capital and motivating their financial institutions and commercial banks to do so. Venture capital disbursement over the countries can be seen through Table 5.2.

Table 5.2: Venture Capital Disbursements (2001)

($ Million)

Country	*Investment*	*No. of Recipient Companies*
Japan	1,858	39
India	1,105	91
South Korea	1,054	19
Singapore	965	26
Australia	548	81
China	393	11
Hong Kong	263	23

Source: Nasscom (2001).

Contrary to the US where the primary and venture capital markets provide most of the Development fund for biotech research, government sponsored research is a major component in Europe and even more important in Asia, with Singapore and India revealing government as the largest investors in the sector. Availability of funding for start-ups has been identified as a key issue for the promotion of biotechnology activities in India. According to the industry, business plans of the present players call for an investment in the region of US$ 500 million, of which only $ 100 million have been tied from various sources. Promoter equity and venture capital assistance from Indian financial institutions account for a large share of the assistance at present. The principal institutions in the sector have been venture capital arms of Indian financial institutions, notably ICICI Ventures, ICF Ventures, UTI Ventures, and SIDBI. Venture capital assistance, estimated to be less than $ 10 million until 2001, have been much below expectations. Reasons for the low interest level by private and overseas venture funds include a rationalization of exposure after the dotcom bust, and the inherently "high- risk" perception of biotech research, given its open-ended revenue models that make purely commercial decisions difficult. Also, in India, biotechnology was still shrouded in controversies regarding its benefits and ethical aspects. Sartorius Ag, Germany is among the larger venture investors in India, and has invested US$ 0.75 million in biotech start-ups, and has also announced stakes in a biotechnology park in Tamil Nadu.

Nevertheless, VCs must generate returns of nearly 25 to 30 per cent compounded year-to-year, and need enough exit routes from some investments. This requires a robust market where VCs can funnel funds into several funds, and exit at appropriate stages from some of their investments. The solution lies in providing tax incentives for investing in BT through tax holidays and pass-through status for venture funds.

6

Profiles of Major Venture Capital Funds and Biotech Companies

1. APIDC-Venture Capital Limited

Andhra Pradesh Industrial Development Corporation (APIDC) promoted APIDC-Venture Capital Limited (VCL) on 29th August 1989. The approval of the Government of India to commence operations was accorded in April 1990. APIDC-VCL was privatized in 1994 and Dynam ventures, East Pvt. Ltd, has been awarded control of APIDC-VCL after a competitive selection process. Thus it has become a subsidiary of Dyman Venture East Pvt. Ltd., a firm promoted by professionals with a wealth of experience in entrepreneurship, consulting, equity investments, technology development, etc.

The company acts as manager and trustee to the APIDC Venture Capital Fund (VCF), 1990. It is the first state level Venture Capital fund in India to be managed by owner-managers with strong entrepreneurial skills. The fund managers' strength is their understanding of what conceiving and building a business or enterprise is all about, having gone through the process themselves.

Initially it was incorporated with an authorized capital of Rs. 2 million, out of which Rs. 2755 million was paid-up capital in 1989. The paid up capital was raised to the level of authorized capital of Rs. 2 million during 1991-92.

The company manages the venture fund of Rs.135 million. The authorized corpus capital of the fund is Rs.135 million out of which Rs. 41.35 million is paid-up, which forms the corpus of the fund known as 'APIDC Venture Capital Fund-1990'. The fund resources come from the World Bank (WB), the Industrial Development Bank of India (IDBI), the Andhra Pradesh Industrial Development Corporation (APIDC), Small Industrial Industrial Development Bank of India (SIDBI), Andhra Bank (AB), Indian Overseas Bank (IOB) and NRIs etc.

APIDC-VCL is the first of series of venture capital funds that will invests in companies in Southern and Western India, with a focus on the state of Andhra Pradesh. It will invest across several business sectors, with projections that seek to exploit key differentials (in market potential, technology, operations, and return on capital) between India and industrialized world. Generally it will invest in start-up as well as expansion type of projects.

Affiliates

Andhra Pradesh Industrial Development Corporation (APIDC), a state owned institution promoting industrial development, has an excellent track record of promoting and nurturing industrial development. The fund can draw on APIDC's rich and varied experience and government connectivity to assist start-up venture as well as those with expansion plans. APIDC a state-owned institution promoting industrial development has an excellent track record of promoting and nurturing industrial development.

Objectives

APIDC has been encouraging technology based ventures in the state of Andhra Pradesh particularly those started by first generation technocrat-entrepreneurs, through equity participation and by canalizing IDBI's seed capital assistance to entrepreneurs. However the main objectives of the fund are:

(1) To promote high technology and assist entrepreneurs to take up ventures involving high risk.

(2) To generate the highest long-term capital gains for its investors, who view their investments as 'patience' money, and

(3) To make its commitment to the enterprises it assist beyond mere funding i.e. assisting and adding values to them in every way it can.

Investment Strategy

APIDC-VCL will invest in companies with the ability to build unique competitive advantages that others will find difficult to emulate. It will add value to portfolio companies through support in activities external to the company, being a responsive facilitator of the entrepreneurial process.

Investment Size

APIDC-VCL is mandated to restrict its investment to Rs. 200 lakhs per round of investment. However, it has successfully syndicated large investments with other venture capital/private equity funds. This funding will be in the form of equity or quasi-equity investment.

Instruments of Finance

APIDC-VCL is using equity shares, redeemable preference shares, convertible debt and conditional loan as instruments for its venture capital finance.

Ideal Client

Ideal client would be able to clearly define the task that is set upon, have a burning desire to succeed, and the perseverance to seek a task to its completion. In the company could be operation in any industrial sector, and the enterprise should be privately held. It would expect its client to have demonstrable integrity, and the ability to build competitive advantages for the company.

Geographical Focus

APIDC-VCL will focus attention on projects in Andhra Pradesh, Karnataka, Maharashtra and Tamil Nadu. Ideally, we would like to fund companies that are located within an hour flight or an overnight journey from Hyderabad or Chennai.

Strength of APIDC-VCL

Entrepreneurial Edge

APIDC-VCL has developed to a fine skill, the ability to recognize the potential of a great entrepreneurial idea, understand it, and gauge its true worth.

Quick Response Time

APIDC-VCL understands how critical reaction time is to the entrepreneur. Its flat organization structure results in quicker decision-making. In projects it associate with, the entrepreneur is relieved of the trauma that on normally goes through in an interface with a funding institution or a development agency. It follows a clearly defined decision-making process that works with clock-like precision. This means that if it agrees on a funding schedule, entrepreneur can count on them to stick to it.

Freedom of Operation

APIDC-VCL strikes the right balance between value-added guidance and providing enterprises adequate freedom to operate without interference. It realizes that every business has its ups and downs. In this regard to realize entrepreneurs' full potential it can assist or guide.

Technology Tie-ups

APIDC-VCL identifies and explores high-potential opportunities that entrepreneurs can use to advantage. It facilitates access to sophisticated technologies for Indian entrepreneurs through links with technical institutions in India and abroad and affects technical alliances through connections with corporate, research institutions, and technology innovators in the west.

Strengths of the Private and Public Sector

APIDC-VCL is the first effectively privatized financial institution in India. With 51 per cent stake ceded to the private sector. This has created a 'Hybrid', which combines the strengths of both the private sector and the public sector.

Asset Managers

It is one of less than handful off Asset Managers, which are owner-manager driven. Most of other Asset Managers and large hierarchical structures dominated by a big institution. Unlike the 'effective' model successful in the developed market, the Asset management team has impressive credentials, strengths in business building, entrepreneurship and strong overseas capabilities that are essential in today's liberalized markets, rather than pure financial skills. This experience allows APIDC-VCL to better relate to better assess and value-add to investee companies.

Organizational Structure

APIDC-VCL is structured on the lines of a tight-knit owner-managed company. Its flat organization structure has a managing director and three executive directors. Four executives and support staff supports them. The responsibility for asset management is distributed either by function or by specific deals.

Management Team

The management team of APIDC-VCL comprises 5 members. They are:

(1) **Sarath Naru**, Managing Director

B.Tech from IIT, Madras and MBA from University of Chicago. Founder-president of a US$ 3 million investment group. Mr. Naru has rich experience in start-up projects. He has earlier worked with Proctor and Gamble as a Brand Manager in the USA and UK.

(2) **D.B.Reddy**, Director

M.Com, M.B.A and CAIIB. Currently Managing Director of Vijay Growth Financial Services Ltd., a leading Merchant Banker in the State of Andhra Pradesh. Mr. Reddy has 20 years experience in venture capital, merchant banking and commercial banking operations. Mr. Reddy is also a consultant with the World Bank.

(3) **Raghuveer Mendu**, Director

B.Tech from IIT Madras and MBA from University of Michigan. Mr. Mendu's area of expertise is information technology and banking. He is the founder and co-chariman of International Designs a Los Angles-based software and systems integration company. He has earlier held senior management positions in US firms specialising in computers and information technology.

(4) **Ajay Khanna**, Director

MS from Virginia Tech and Ph.D. from Cornell University, New York. A specialist in operations management. Mr. Khanna is currently working for Morgan Stanely, New York. He also served as Assistant Professor (Operations Management) at the Graduate School of Business, New York University.

(5) **A.Ramesh**, Vice-President

A Chemical Engineer from Regional Engineering College, Warangal, AP and an MBA from IIM, Bangalore. Mr. Ramesh has experience in the areas of design R&D production and general management in the areas of chemicals, polymers, drugs and project appraisals etc. for over 15 years.

Deal Generation

VCL deal generation strategy will produce a relatively higher level of quality deals than a general promotional approach, and will generate sufficient deals to invest the monies raised by it. Their focused approach to canvassing entrepreneurs will be more efficient in finding qualified entrepreneurs and project ideas that meet their criteria of 'Key differentials'. VCL has set up a flow of investment opportunities with its existing network in India and with its associated in the USA. VCL also plans to promote through focused seminars, a public relations campaign to institutions and industry associations, to heighten the awareness of its activities.

Investment Decision Making Steps

VCL has set up a responsive system of receiving the investment proposals, evaluating them and communicate to the promoters/ entrepreneurs. This is basically a four-step process:

(1) The submission of a full-fledged business plan with all supporting evidence,
(2) A full blown presentation by the management team,
(3) Final completion of the due diligence, and
(4) Negotiation of the terms of investment.

The promoters/entrepreneurs are made fully aware of these steps and at each stage they are informed whether the process has moved forward or the proposal is being rejected.

Due Diligence and Criteria for Investment

VCL will evaluate each deal against the started 'investment strategy', and whether the returns meet the target rates, and the risks can be contained and are appropriate, prior to proceeding further. Specifically, VCL will evaluate:

(1) The quality of the management team;
(2) The match with our strategy of 'Key differentials' resulting in a strong competitive edge for the company;
(3) The size and growth rate of the market;
(4) Potential for high profitability while protecting the downside;
(5) Types of risk and their management; and

(6) The ability to disinvest with high capital gains and the congruence of these objectives with the management teams.

Monitoring and Value Addition

VCL, in line with its pro-active strategy of value-addition, follows an active mode of monitoring and value addition. Specifically, VCL in collaboration with the investee company sets up milestones that lead up to the eventual disinvestments from the investee company. These milestones are then monitored actively, and the invested company is urged to adopt a reporting system that facilitates the monitoring of the progress versus the milestones. At least one member from VCL will typically serve on the Board of Directors of the company on the average of once in a week, and will install a reporting system that evaluates progress of the investee company versus the milestone every month.

Value-Addition: APIDC-VCL's Philosophy

VCL believes in value-addition. In the quality of service they render to their clients. More comprehensively, and in time. So what sets them apart from other venture capital funds? VCL can attract the best deals, and build investee companies better, because of its network of international affiliates. VCL, with its merchant banking affiliation, can not only manage assets, but also evolve exit strategies for investors. VCL enjoys a strategic location, as Andhra Pradesh holds great promise for enterprise promotion. VCL draws on its government connectivity to add value to the process of enterprise building.

Exit: Easy for the Investor

VCL will develop financial packages for the investee companies in such a manner that exit by IPO, or through partial sale to overseas corporations is easily available to overseas investors. Thus, investors will be in a relationship with VCL that is not only mutually beneficial but also convenient.

APIDC-VCL's Competitive Advantage

APIDC-VCL's competitive advantage is caused by:

(1) Unique Owner-Manager structure proven the most successful in the World, will enable APIDC-C/VCL to build a better venture capital company,
(2) International affiliations and network to add value to invested companies and to able attract the best deals,
(3) Unique affiliation with Government best utilizes the strengths of the Govt. in terms of help the investee companies when needed,
(4) Merchant Bank affiliation helps current asset management and exit strategy execution.

Terms and Conditions for Equity Participation

The terms and conditions of APIDC-VCL for equity participation are as follows:

(1) The company shall carry out such alterations to its Memorandum and the Articles of Association in consultation with and to the satisfaction of APIDC-VCL so as to safeguard the interests of APIDC-VCL arising out of its assistance granted to the company.
(2) The company/promoters shall enter into a suitable investment agreement with APIDC-VCL to the satisfaction of APIDC-VCL.
(3) The company shall produce permission/clearance from the appropriate government agency for setting up the unit.
(4) The company shall raise its authorized capital upto Rs. 50.00 lakhs.
(5) The subscribed share capital of the company shall be Rs. 44.10 lakhs.
(6) The contribution of the private promoters shall not be less than Rs. 30.20 lakhs in the equity share capital of the company. The contribution by the APIDC-VCL shall be made on pro-rata basis with that of the contribution of the promoters and their associated in the equity share

capital of the company after obtaining necessary clearances from financial institutions and do their government agencies. APIDC-VCL shall release its share of contribution only after the shares subscribed and paid up to the extent of 100 per cent of its promoters' contribution towards equity of the company.

(7) The promoter directors shall give an undertaking to the APIDC-VCL in such form as may be prescribed by the APIDC-VCL that they shall procure for the company such additional finances as may be required to meet the shortfall, if any, in financing the project and/or for working capita. The funds brought in shall not be withdrawn without the prior approval of APIDC-VCL.

(8) The company/promoter directors shall make necessary arrangements to the satisfaction of APIDC-VCL for raising a term loan to the extent of Rs. 102.90 lakhs required for financing the project from Banks/other financial institutions.

(9) The company/promoters directors shall not raise any further term loans/deposits other than the amount of Rs. 102.90 lakhs as mentioned above except with the specific written approval of the APIDC-VCL.

(10) It shall be the responsibility of the company to raise short-term borrowings from scheduled bank for working capital requirements of the company.

(11) The actual expenditure incurred by the promoters for the projects shall be subject to the scrutiny an approval of the APIDC-VCL.

(12) The company shall not without the proper consent and written approval of the APIDC-VCL pay any commission to its promoter directors or concerns in which directors are interested and for furnishing guarantees for any financial assistance obtained by the company for the purpose of its project.

(13) The company shall broadbase the Board and finalizes the composition of its Board of Directors to the satisfaction of the APIDC-VCL.

(14) APIDC-VCL shall have the right to appoint and remove from time to time director(s) on the Board of Directors of the company; such director(s) is (are) hereinafter referred to as 'Nominee Director(s), so long as the APIDC-VCL holds shares in the equity as a result of direct subscription.

(15) The number of directors to represent APIDC-VCL on the company Board shall be in promotion to the APIDC-VCL's shareholding in the company with a minimum of one directior and the APIDC-VCL's nominess shall not be required to hold any qualification shares.

(16) At least one of the nominess of the APIDC-VCL shall be non-rational director. The articles of association of the company shall contain suitable provisions in this behalf. If at any time, the Nominee Director is not able to attend a meeting of the Board of Directors or any of its Committees, of which he is a member, APIDC-VCL may depute an Observer to attend the meeting. The expenses incurred by APIDC-VCL in this connection shall be borne by the company.

(17) Provided however, APIDC-VCL shall have the liberty and discretion to appoint such directors immediately after the acceptance of the letter of intent by the company, but such appointment shall not be construed as any commitment on the part of the APIDC-VCL to disburse the financial assistance unless the APIDC-VCL is fully satisfied that the company has compiled with all the stipulated terms and conditions precedent to such disbursement.

(18) The Managing Director of the company shall be the nominee of the promoter of the company who shall be appointed to the satisfaction of the APIDC-VCL.

(19) The APIDC-VCL reserves to itself the right to inspect the factory, properties and assets, documents and record, books and accounts etc of the company during the period the APIDC-VCL holds shares in the company.

(20) The company shall keep the APIDC-VCL informed in such manner and in such forms as may be prescribed by the APIDC-VCL from time to time of the progress made in the implementation of the project and of the working of the same and also of any expenditure/ diversification thereof, as long as the APIDC-VCL holds any shares in the company. The company shall furnish to the APIDC-VCL all additional information, data, documents and explanations as may be called by the APIDC-VCL in relation to the working and affairs.

(21) The company shall furnish to the APIDC-VCL all notices in respect of the Board Meetings, shareholders meetings of the company together with notes and minutes of thereof in addition to the circulation of the same to the nominees of the APIDC-VCL on the Board of the company.

(22) The Management of the company vest in the Board of Directors and the day-to-day affairs shall be entrusted to the Managing Director/Committee of Directors.

(23) The promoter directors shall not transfer, dispose off or pledge or in any way encumber their shareholdings in the company without the prior consent and written approval of the APIDC-VCL and the company shall not recognize or register any such transfer of shares without the consent of the APIDC-VCL.

(24) The company shall issue the share certificates to the APIDC-VCL in marketable lots for the subscription made by it towards the equity share capital of the company.

(25) All the matters relating to the affairs of the company and the project such as capital expenditure raising loans, awarding contracts, placement of orders for goods and services etc. shall be decided by the APIDC-VCL on the Board of Directors of the company or a Committee of Directors consisting of the APIDC-VCL's nominee(s) and the Managing Director of the company and any other directors of the company.

Contributors to Fund

The contributors of APIDC-VCL fund are All India Financial Institutions, State level financial institutions, Nationalized banks/SBIs , Multilateral Development Agencies, Private sector, Non-resident Indians and Public. The sources of funds of APIDC-VCL are shown in table.

Table 6.1: Contributors to APIDC-VCL's Fund

Contributories to fund	*Amount (Rs. million)*
All India Financial Institutions (IDBI)	30.00
State Level Institutions (APIDC)	22.50
Andhra Bank	15.00
Private-Sector Companies	2.50
World Bank	20.00
Others	45.00
Total	**135.00**

Source: Annual Reports of APIDC-VCL

Table shows that the sources of funds of APIDC-VCL so far. It has mobilised Rs. 30 million from All India Financial Institutions (IDBI) followed by Rs. 22.50 million from State Level Financial Institutions (APIDC), Rs.15 million from Andhra Bank, Rs. 2.50 from private sector companies, Rs. 20 million from World Bank and Rs. 45 million from other sources.

Table 6.2: Sectoral Dispersal

Information Technology	22
Agro-Food	110
Chemicals, Drugs, Pharmaceuticals, Basic Chemicals	180
Mineral Based	85
Engineering, Metallurgical, Electrical, Electronics, etc.	189
Textiles, Jute, Silk, etc.	77
Paper, Paper Board	42
Rubber, Leather, Hotels, etc.	103
Total	**808**

Source: Annual Reports of the Company.

It is evident from the table that the APIDC-VCL fund has catalyzed a total industrial investment of about Rs. 5,488 crores in 808 industrial units. Out of it a significant amount has been flown into Engineering, Metallurgical, Electrical, Electronics, Rubber, Leather, Hotels, Chemicals and Pharmaceuticals and Agro-Food Companies.

Enriching and Empowering Entrepreneurs

Commercial intelligence relating to various industries is made available to prospective entrepreneurs. APIDC is associated with organizations like FAPCCI, CII, AMIO, HMA, in their Specialized Seminars and Workshops, which are beneficial for the entrepreneurs.

Thrust areas

The new Equity Policy of the Company proposes to give a special impetus to Industrial Development. The Company has identified the following for special focus for investment.

(1) Food and Agro processing except traditional industries.
(2) Petroleum, Petro-chemicals.
(3) Chemicals and Fertilizers.
(4) Engineering and Automotives.
(5) Mineral based industries.
(6) Information Technology.
(7) 100% Export Oriented Units.
(8) Biotechnology.
(9) Renewable sources of Energy.
(10) Energy Saving Devices, Appliances, etc.
(11) Energy Efficient and Waste Reduction Technologies and Processes.
(12) Pollution Control Equipment and Devices.
(13) Waste Utilization and Recycling.

Biotech Investments

APIDC-Venture Capital has put investments of $1.62 million (Rs. 8.1 crore) in three US-Indian biotech companies. In the first batch of funding from its recent Biotech Venture Fund, it has put in $ 5,40,000 each in Bioserve Biotechnologies, Genomik Design Pharma and Silico Insights. The investment through the APIDC-Venture Capital has attracted tremendous response from several banks and insurance companies. So, it planned with a corpus of Rs. 150 crore, and has closed commitments for Rs. 40 crore, including contributions from GIC, LIC, Andhra Bank and the AP Government. The fund has picked start-up and early-stage businesses such as healthcare, drug discovery, agriculture, dairy etc.

2. ICICI Venture Capital Fund

ICICI Venture (formerly TDICI Limited) was founded in 1988 as a joint venture with the Unit Trust of India. Subsequently, ICICI bought out UTI's stake in 1998 and ICICI Venture became a fully owned subsidiary of ICICI. ICICI Venture also has an affiliation with the Trust Company of the West (TCW), which provides it a platform for networking Indian companies with global markets and technology. Strong parentage and affiliates for ICICI Venture also translates into access to a broad spectrum of financial and analytical resources thus enabling a keen understanding of the Indian financial markets and entrepreneurial ethos.

ICICI Venture is the largest and one of the most successful private equity and venture capital management companies in India with aggregate funds under management in excess of USD 650 mn. It is a subsidiary of ICICI Bank, the largest private sector financial services group in India with assets of over USD 30.0 bn (Sep. 2004) and market capitalization of about USD 5.3 bn (Feb. 2005).Over the years, ICICI Venture has built an enviable portfolio of companies in the sectors of information technology, pharmaceuticals, biotechnology, media and retail thereby delivering value consistently to its investors. ICICI Venture has the distinction of managing a large number of exits in the country. With over 100 liquidity events, the organization has reaped rich experience and is well positioned to handle IPOs, strategic sale and/or mergers. It has a wide network of third party investors, which include domestic investors such as public sector banks, financial institutions and insurance companies. A significant portion of the fund's corpus is also from international development financial institutions and international funds. The company has over 40 qualified professionals with experience across sectors and functions. The capabilities of the team, structure of the organization, emphasis on value creation and performance evaluation matrices enable ICICI Venture to extract superior returns from its investments. ICICI Venture is currently investing out of the India Advantage Fund with a corpus of USD 245 mn. The Fund's investment philosophy is to pursue investments in established companies that are leaders or potential leaders in their respective markets and where there is a clear proposition for value creation.

Venture Team

The ICICI Venture team has worked together to build a strong foundation to build a world-class Private Equity enterprise. This involved shaping up current portfolio, planning exits, blueprinting the investment thesis for the new fund, understanding and analyzing sectors to create a shortlist of focus sectors. The collective performance of the team helped in gaining investor confidence culminating in raising the largest domestic fund in India. The details of team members is given below.

Renuka Ramnath, MD and CEO

Renuka Ramnath, Managing Director and CEO, is credited with raising the India Advantage Fund, India's largest private equity fund till date with a corpus of US$ 230 million.The fund is today an investor in some of the most notable transactions in India, including India's first leveraged buyout, first real estate and first mezzanine. Ms. Ramnath is a graduate in Engineering and holds an MBA in Finance from University of Bombay. She also completed the Advanced Management Program at Harvard Business School in May 1999.

Aluri Srinivasa Rao, Director—Investments

Aluri Srinivasa Rao, Director-Investments, spearheads the life sciences business at ICICI Venture focusing on the emerging biotech, restructuring pharma, evolving healthcare and the enabling technology sectors. He brings with him over 13 years of organizational building and corporate experience in India, UK and USA. He is a Sloan fellow and has completed the one-year time program in General Management from London Business School.

Bala Deshpande, Director—Investments

Prior to joining ICICI Venture in 2000, Bala has had over 10 years of cross-function at multiple industries. She has worked in leading MNCs such as International Best Foods, Cadbury and ICICI. At ICICI Venture she is using her industry background and operational experience to identify growth opportunities for investment and to play a strategic role in shaping the future of investee companies. She has been actively involved in companies such as Billjunction Payments Ltd., Naukri.com, Miditech, among others. She is on the board of several successful companies including Shoppers' Stop, Pantaloon Retail and Subhiksha, TV Today etc.

Her private equity experience has seen the full cycle from nurturing young companies to executing over 10 exits including IPOs, buy-back, strategic sale and capital market divestments. She currently heads the growth capital investments group at ICICI Venture, which focuses on providing expansion capital across sectors including retail, media, textiles and manufacturing. In the new fund, India Advantage Fund, She is responsible for the investments in Welspun, Subhiksha and Nagarjuna Construction. Bala is a Master in Economics, Bombay University and Masters in Management Studies, Jamnalal Bajaj Institute of Management Studies.

Beena Chotai, Chief Financial Officer

Beena has been associated with ICICI Venture for over 13 years in various capacities and is currently the Chief Financial Officer of the organization. She is one of the few industry professionals in India to have handled all the stages of the life cycle of a venture capital fund. She has been involved in setting up and structuring exits of several domestic and cross border funds and is also credited with the restructuring of a cross border fund having investments in various countries, an assignment that was a first of its kind.

She has played an active role in defining and shaping the regulatory environment of the industry and is credited for a number of measures introduced by the regulators to encourage the industry. She has participated in the Dr. Lahiri committee set up by SEBI to recommend changes to the regulatory environment of the industry and has made representations to several regulatory authorities including SEBI, RBI and CBDT. Currently, she is overseeing the accounting, taxation, treasury, HR and Admin and capital market functions and is actively involved in the monitoring process of portfolio companies.

Devaiah P.M., General Counsel

Devaiah currently heads the Legal and Compliance function of ICICI Venture with over 14 years of Corporate Law experience. Since joining ICICI Venture in 2002 he has been involved in a wide range of corporate law assignments such as negotiating joint ventures, structuring private equity deals, negotiating shareholders agreements, handling high stake litigations, acquisitions and mergers, international arbitrations, international vendor contracts, technology transfer arrangements, IPR related matters, handling legal due diligence, to name a few. Located in Bangalore, Devaiah serves on the board of Infomedia India Limited, a listed company, ICLC and various other SPV's. He has worked with companies in variety of industries, with focus on Services, Manufacturing, Private Equity, Telecom, IT and Power.

Prior to joining ICICI Venture, Devaiah worked with the BPL Cellular, the Carlyle Group, Levers, and TATA Projects. At BPL and Carlyle Group he headed the Legal function. Devaiah is a commerce graduate and received his master's degree in Law from the University of Mysore, India.

Jayanta Banerjee, Director—Investments

Jayanta has been with ICICI Venture since 2002 and has over 13 years of industry experience including in the area of Investment Banking and entrepreneurship. He brings a blend of experience of the Indian capital markets, skills of financial structuring and negotiations as well as the perspective of an entrepreneur in understanding of businesses. Jayanta is an engineer from Jadavpur University and an MBA from IIM Bangalore.

Kishore Gotety, Director—Investments

Kishore's experience in Investment Banking with the ICICI Bank group has helped in raising the largest domestic fund-in India. He has another first to his credit viz. accessing debt markets for structured paper and tapped the bank markets successfully for selling corporate loans for ICICI. He has a thorough understanding of the capital markets in India and closely tracks the market developments internationally. In his current role in ICICI Venture he heads the Mezzanine investment practice.

Ravindra K, Chief Risk Officer

Ravindra joined ICICI Venture in September 2000. He is currently responsible for assessing and mitigating business risks in ICICI Venture's existing and potential investments, and works closely with the Investment teams to maximize the returns from the investment portfolio. He also manages some of ICICI Venture's earlier investments in the areas of Information Technology (IT) related services, IT enabled services, and Small and Medium Enterprises (SME) segments.

Prior to joining ICICI Venture, Ravindra worked with the erstwhile ICICI Ltd. (since merged with ICICI Bank) for over 12 years in the corporate credit function. His responsibilities at ICICI included developing and maintaining client relationships in a wide range of industries, cross selling ICICI Group products, working out innovative financing solutions for clients, restructuring stressed assets, etc. He has handled both equity and debt related products during his tenure at ICICI, and headed ICICI's Hyderabad Zonal office before moving to ICICI Venture in September 2000. Ravindra holds a Bachelors degree in Mechanical Engineering from the Indian Institute of Technology, Madras, and an MBA from the Indian Institute of Management, Calcutta.

Sanjay Mehrottra, Head—Capital Markets

Sanjay brings with him over 15 years of experience in the Indian Equity Markets. he is currently responsible for advising on the divestment of the listed companies in the portfolio's and also advising on the timing of the IPO's. He would be responsible for developing relations with foreign Institutional Investor's and other market intermediaries in the capital market and be a investor relations personnel for the HNI clients. Sanjay is a Commerce Graduate and has done his Masters in Management Studies from Mumbai University.

Sudhir Variyar, Director—Investments

Sudhir brings a well rounded financial service perspective having worked in investment banking, structured finance, corporate finance and credit rating. He started his career in ICICI Securities, the investment banking subsidiary of ICICI Bank where he was responsible for equity and debt syndication for companies in the oil and gas sector. Subsequently he was part of the team that set-up the structured finance business of ICICI Bank. Thereafter, he worked in corporate finance at Enron India and BPL Cellular.

Prior to joining ICICI Venture, he was Senior Director at Fitch Ratings where he was a key member of the India team.

Specifically, he was responsible for developing the structured finance business from scratch to a position of leadership. Sudhir is a chemical engineer from the Institute of Technology, Banaras Hindu University, and an MBA from the Indian Institute of Management, Kolkata.

Sumit Chandwani, Director—Investments

Sumit brings with him over 13 years of private equity, structured finance and project finance experience. Since joining ICICI Venture in 2000 he has been involved in all aspects of investment process; including sourcing, transaction structuring, financing and execution of post closing growth strategies. Located in Mumbai, Sumit serves on the board of PVR Limited, Creative Eye Ltd. and Accel ICIM Ltd. He has worked with companies in variety of industries, with focus on pharmaceutical, services, media and manufacturing. He was responsible for making investments in PVR Ltd, Samtel Color and Infowavz and engineered exits in Infowavz, Medicorp, Biocon and Accel ICIM. He is the fund manager for TCW/ICICI fund based out of Mauritius. He currently heads the Buyout practice for ICICI Venture.

Portfolio of ICICI

ICICI Venture has built a diverse portfolio of companies in different industries and at various stages of their life cycle. It has consistently identified high-growth sectors early on and supported strong management teams with compelling value propositions. The following are various industries in which ICICI Venture has put its hands.

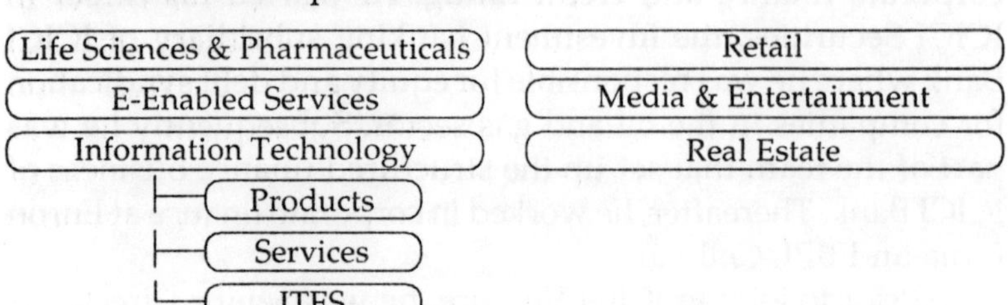

Figure 6.1

ICICI Venture has floated several Funds successfully till date with total assets under management in excess of USD 400 million, they are:

(1) ICICI Eco-Net Fund
(2) ICICI Equity Fund
(3) India Advantage Fund
(4) ICICI Emerging Sectors Fund
(5) ICICI Software Fund
(6) TCW/ICICI Funds

Financial Performance

Financial year 2002-03 was a landmark year for ICICI Venture. ICICI Venture raised the largest Indian Private Equity Fund and also engineered effective exits and enhanced the value of its existing portfolio. ICICI Venture Funds launched four new domestic funds whereas six existing funds under management were either liquidated or were in the process of liquidation. The most significant achievement of ICICI Venture was the successful First Closing of the Rs. 750 billion India Advantage Fund launched this year. List of Biotech companies financed by ICICI Venture fund and history of ICICI can be seen from Tables 6.3 and 6.4 respectively.

Table 6.3: List of Biotech Companies financed by ICICI Venture Fund

Company	*Activity*
Syngene	Indl. Enzymes and CRO
Strand Genomics	Bio informatics
Avesthagen	Start up in Agri genetics, contract research
Microplantae	Tissue Culture
Gum India	
Bangalore Genei (P) Ltd	Restriction enzymes
Vimta Labs	Services/Testing Lab moving into biotech services.

Source: ICICI website

Table 6.4: History of ICICI at a Glance

1955:	The Industrial Credit and Investment Corporation of India Limited (ICICI) incorporated at the initiative of the World Bank, the Government of India and representatives of Indian industry, with the objective of creating a development financial institution for providing medium-term and long-term project financing to Indian businesses. Mr. A. Ramaswami Mudaliar elected as the first Chairman of ICICI Limited ICICI emerges as the major source of foreign currency loans to Indian industry. Besides funding from the World Bank and other multilateral agencies, ICICI also among the first Indian companies to raise funds from International markets.
1956:	ICICI declared its first Dividend at 3.5%.
1958:	Mr. G.L. Mehta was appointed the 2nd Chairman of ICICI Ltd.
1960:	ICICI building at 163, Backbay Reclamation was inaugurated.
1961:	The first West German loan of DM 5 million from Kredianstalt was obtained by ICICI.
1967:	ICICI made its first debenture issue for Rs. 6 crore, which was over subscribed.
1969:	First two regional offices in Calcutta and Madras were opened.
1972:	Second entity in India to set-up merchant banking services. Mr. H.T. Parekh appointed as the third Chairman of ICICI.
1977:	ICICI sponsors the formation of Housing Development Finance Corporation. Managed its first equity public issue.
1978:	Mr. James Raj appointed as the fourth Chairman of ICICI.
1979:	Mr. Siddharth Mehta appointed as the fifth Chairman of ICICI.
1982:	Becomes the first ever Indian borrower to raise European Currency Units. ICICI commences leasing business.
1984:	Mr. S. Nadkarni appointed as the sixth Chairman of ICICI.
1985:	Mr.N.Vaghul appointed as the seventh Chairman and Managing Director of ICICI.
1986:	ICICI first Indian Institution to receive ADB Loans. First public issue by an Indian entity in the Swiss Capital Markets. ICICI along with UTI sets up Credit Rating Information Services of India Limited, (CRISIL) India's first professional credit rating agency. ICICI promotes Shipping Credit and Investment Company of India Limited. (SCICI) The Corporation made a public issue of Swiss Franc 75 million in Switzerland, the first public issue by any Indian equity in the Swiss Capital Market.

(contd.)

(contd.)

1987: ICICI signed a loan agreement for Sterling Pound 10 million with Commonwealth Development Corporation (CDC), the first loan by CDC for financing projects in India.

1988: ICICI promotes TDICI - India's first venture capital company.

1993: ICICI sets-up ICICI Securities and Finance Company Limited in joint venture with J. P. Morgan.
ICICI sets up ICICI Asset Management Company.

1994: ICICI sets up ICICI Bank.

1996: ICICI becomes the first company in the Indian financial sector to raise GDR.
ICICI announces merger with SCICI.
Mr.K.V.Kamath appointed the Managing Director and CEO of ICICI Ltd.

1997: ICICI was the first intermediary to move away from single prime rate to three-tier prime rates structure and introduced yield-curve based pricing.
The name "The Industrial Credit and Investment Corporation of India Limited " was changed to "ICICI Limited".
ICICI announces takeover of ITC Classic Finance.

1998: Introduced the new logo symbolizing a common corporate identity for the ICICI Group.
ICICI announces takeover of Anagram Finance.

1999: ICICI launches retail finance - car loans, house loans and loans for consumer durables.
ICICI becomes the first Indian Company to list on the NYSE through an issue of American Depositary Shares.

2000: ICICI Bank becomes the first commercial bank from India to list its stock on NYSE.
ICICI Bank announces merger with Bank of Madura.

2001: The Boards of ICICI Ltd and ICICI Bank approved the merger of ICICI with ICICI Bank.

2002: Moodys' assign higher than sovereign rating to ICICI.
Merger of ICICI Limited, ICICI Capital Sercvices Ltd and ICICI Personal Financial Services Limited with ICICI Bank.

Source: ICICI website

IDBI Profile

The genesis of "Industrial Development Bank of India Limited" (IDBI Ltd.) can be traced to the establishment of The Industrial Development Bank of India (IDBI), its predecessor entity, in 1964, by an Act of Parliament to provide credit and other facilities for the development of industry. IDBI's charter was later broad-based to also encompass the responsibilities of principal financial institution for co-ordinating the working of National and State-level institutions engaged in financing, promoting and developing industry. Initially set up as a fully-owned subsidiary of the Reserve Bank of India (RBI), the ownership of IDBI was later transferred to the Government of India in 1976. Although Government shareholding in the Bank came down below 100 per cent following IDBI's public issue in July 1995, the former continues to be the major shareholder (current shareholding: 51.4%).

During the four decades of its existence, IDBI has been instrumental not only in establishing a well-developed, diversified and efficient industrial and institutional structure but also adding a qualitative dimension to the process of industrial development in the country. Cumulative assistance sanctioned and disbursed by IDBI since inception up to end-September 2004 aggregated around Rs. 2,23,000 crore and Rs. 1,78,000 crore respectively. IDBI's asset base stood in the vicinity of Rs. 63,850 crore at end-September 2004.

As a considered response to changes in its operating environment following initiation of reforms since the early nineties and the resultant concerns of IDBI's sustained viability therein in its current avatar, IDBI, in consultation with the Government of India, decided to transform into a commercial bank without eschewing its secular development finance obligations. The migration to the new business model of commercial banking, with its gateway to low-cost current/savings bank deposits, it was felt, would help overcome most of the limitations of the current business model of development finance while simultaneously enabling it to diversify its client/asset base. Towards this end, the IDBI (Transfer of Undertaking and Repeal) Act, 2003 was passed by Parliament on December 16, 2003 and received the President's assent on December 30, 2003. The provisions of the Act came into force from July 2, 2004 in terms of a Government Notification to this effect. The Notification enabled IDBI to obtain the requisite statutory and regulatory approvals, including those from RBI, for conversion into a banking company. The new company viz. "Industrial

Development Bank of India Limited" (IDBIL) was incorporated on September 27, 2004 and the Registrar of Companies, Mumbai, issued the certificate for commencement of business to IDBI Ltd. on September 28, 2004. Subsequently, the Central Government notified October 1, 2004 as the 'Appointed Date' and RBI issued the requisite notification on September 30, 2004 incorporating IDBI Ltd. as a 'scheduled bank' under the RBI Act, 1934. Consequently, IDBI, the erstwhile Development Financial Institution of the country, formally entered the portals of banking business as IDBI Ltd. from October 1, 2004, over and above the business currently being transacted.

IDBI Ltd. is registered as a company under the Companies Act, 1956 to carry out banking business in accordance with the provisions of the Banking Regulation Act, 1949. The IDBI Repeal Act, 2003 enabled IDBI to become a banking company without the need to obtain a separate banking licence under the Banking Regulation Act, 1949. IDBI Ltd. will enjoy certain regulatory forbearance, including exemption from compliance with SLR requirements (mandated under the Banking Regulation Act) for the first five years. All existing shareholders of the erstwhile IDBI, including the Central Government, have become pro-rata shareholders of IDBI Ltd. from the 'appointed date'. Further, the provisions of the Memorandum and Articles of Association of IDBI Ltd. require that the Central Government, as a shareholder of the Company, shall, at all times, maintain not less than 51 per cent of the issued capital of the company.

The authorized capital of IDBI Ltd. has been reduced to Rs.1250 crore from Rs.1500 crore (the authorized capital of erstwhile IDBI) in conformity with the provision of the Banking Regulation Act. The paid-up capital of the Company, at Rs. 653 crore, however, remains the same as the paid-up capital of the erstwhile IDBI.

Products and Services of IDBI

The erstwhile IDBI has played a pioneering role in fulfilling its mission of promoting industrial growth through financing of medium and long-term projects, in consonance with national plans and priorities. Over the years, IDBI has enlarged its basket of products and services to industrial concerns, covering almost the entire spectrum of industrial activities, including manufacturing and services. IDBI and its successor entity IDBI Ltd. provides financial assistance, both in rupee and foreign currencies, for green-field projects as also for expansion, modernization and diversification purposes.

Further, in order to cater to the diverse and customized needs of its corporate clients, IDBI Ltd. has structured suitable products like equipment finance, asset credit, corporate loan, working capital loan and bills discounting to variously finance acquisition of equipment and capital assets, besides meeting capital expenditure and/or incremental long-term working capital requirements. It also offers structured products like lines of credit to meet the funding requirements for execution of turnkey contracts. Besides, IDBI Ltd. provides a wide array of fee-based services.

IDBI Ltd. also provides indirect financial assistance through refinancing of loans extended by State-level financial institutions and banks and by way of rediscounting of bills of exchange arising out of sale of indigenous machinery on deferred payment terms. Not only that, in recent past IDBI has also started its Venture Capital Fund to cater the financial needs of reward building entrepreneurs having good knowledge and skills in creativity and technology.

IDBI Venture Capital Fund

This was established in 1986 with an objective to finance the projects whose requirements range between Rs.5 lakhs to Rs. 2.5 crores. The pomoters' stake should be at least 10 per cent for the ventures below Rs.50 lakhs and 15 per cent for those above 50 lakhs. Financial assistance is extended in the form of unsecured loans involving minimum legal formalities. Interest at a concessional rate of 9 per cent is charged during technology development and trial run of production stage and it will be 17 per cent once the product is commercially traded in the market by the financially assisted firm. IDBI venture capital fund extends its financial assistance to the ventures likely to be engaged in the fields of chemicals, computer softwares, electronics, biotechnology, non-conventional energy, food products, refractories and medical equipments. List of Biotech companies financed can be seen from the Table 6.5.

Table 6.5: List of Biotech Companies financed by IDBI Venture Fund

Company	*Institutions*	*Activity*
Bharat Biotech	TDB. IDBI-VCF.	Hepatitis-B. Re combinant
	Unlisted	make. Valued at over Rs. 200 crores.
Vimta Labs	ICICI-VCF. IDBI. Listed	Services/Testing Lab moving into biotech services.

Source: IDBI website

Milestones of IDBI

- **July 1964:** Set up under an Act of Parliament as a wholly-owned subsidiary of Reserve Bank of India.
- **February 1976:** Ownership transferred to Government of India. Designated Principal Financial Institution for co-ordinating the working of institutions at national and State levels engaged in financing, promoting and developing industry.
- **March 1982:** International Finance Division of IDBI transferred to Export-Import Bank of India, established as a wholly-owned corporation of Government of India, under an Act of Parliament.
- **April 1990:** Set up Small Industries Development Bank of India (SIDBI) under SIDBI Act as a wholly-owned subsidiary to cater to specific needs of small-scale sector. In terms of an amendment to SIDBI Act in September 2000, IDBI divested 51 per cent of its shareholding in SIDBI in favour of banks and other institutions in the first phase. IDBI has subsequently divested 79.13 per cent of its stake in its erstwhile subsidiary to date.
- **January 1992:** Accessed domestic retail debt market for the first time with innovative Deep Discount Bonds; registered path-breaking success.

- **December 1993:** Set up IDBI Capital Market Services Ltd. as a wholly-owned subsidiary to offer a broad range of financial services, including Bond Trading, Equity Broking, Client Asset Management and Depository Services. IDBI Capital is currently a leading Primary Dealer in the country.
- **September 1994:** Set up IDBI Bank Ltd. in association with SIDBI as a private sector commercial bank subsidiary, a sequel to RBI's policy of opening up domestic banking sector to private participation as part of overall financial sector reforms.
- **October 1994:** IDBI Act amended to permit public ownership upto 49 per cent.
- **July 1995:** Made Initial Public Offer of Equity and raised over Rs.2000 crore, thereby reducing Government stake to 72.14 per cent.
- **March 2000:** Entered into a JV agreement with Principal Financial Group, USA for participation in equity and management of IDBI Investment Management Company Ltd., erstwhile a 100 per cent subsidiary. IDBI divested its entire shareholding in its asset management venture in March 2003 as part of overall corporate strategy.
- **March 2000:** Set up IDBI Intech Ltd. as a wholly-owned subsidiary to undertake IT-related activities.
- **June 2000:** A part of Government shareholding converted to preference capital, since redeemed in March 2001; Government stake currently 58.47 per cent.
- **August 2000:** Became the first All-India Financial Institution to obtain ISO 9002:1994 Certification for its treasury operations. Also became the first organisation in Indian financial sector to obtain ISO 9001:2000 Certification for its forex services.
- **March 2001:** Set up IDBI Trusteeship Services Ltd. to provide technology-driven information and professional services to subscribers and issuers of debentures.
- **Feburary 2002:** Associated with select banks/ institutions in setting up Asset Reconstruction

Company (India) Limited (ARCIL), which will be involved with the strategic management of non-performing and stressed assets of Financial Institutions and Banks.

- **September 2003:** IDBI acquired the entire shareholding of Tata Finance Limited in Tata Homefinance Ltd, signalling IDBI's foray into the retail finance sector. The housing finance subsidiary has since been renamed 'IDBI Homefinance Limited'.
- **December 2003:** On December 16, 2003, the Parliament approved The Industrial Development Bank (Transfer of Undertaking and Repeal Bill) 2002 to repeal IDBI Act, 1964. The President's assent for the same was obtained on December 30, 2003. The Repeal Act is aimed at bringing IDBI under the Companies Act for investing it with the requisite operational flexibility to undertake commercial banking business under the Banking Regulation Act, 1949 in addition to the business carried on and transacted by it under the IDBI Act, 1964.
- **July 2004:** The Industrial Development Bank (Transfer of Undertaking and Repeal) Act 2003 came into force from July 2, 2004.
- **July 2004:** The Boards of IDBI and IDBI Bank Ltd. take in-principle decision regarding merger of IDBI Bank Ltd. with proposed Industrial Development Bank of India Ltd. in their respective meetings on July 29, 2004.
- **September 2004:** The Trust Deed for Stressed Assets Stabilisation Fund (SASF) executed by its Trustees on September 24, 2004 and the first meeting of the Trustees was held on September 27, 2004.
- **September 2004:** The new entity "Industrial Development Bank of India" was incorporated on September 27, 2004 and Certificate of commencement of business was issued by the Registrar of Companies on September 28, 2004.
- **September 2004:** Notification issued by Ministry of Finance specifying SASF as a financial institution under Section 2(h)(ii) of Recovery of Debts due to Banks and Financial Institutions Act, 1993.

- **September 2004:** Notification issued by Ministry of Finance on September 29, 2004 for issue of non-interest bearing GoI IDBI Special Security, 2024, aggregating Rs.9000 crore, of 20-year tenure.
- **September 2004:** Notification for appointed day as October 1, 2004, issued by Ministry of Finance on September 29, 2004.
- **September 2004:** RBI issues notification for inclusion of Industrial Development Bank of India Ltd. in Schedule II of RBI Act, 1934 on September 30, 2004.
- **October 2004:** Appointed day—October 01, 2004—Transfer of undertaking of IDBI to IDBI Ltd. IDBI Ltd. commences operations as a banking company. IDBI Act, 1964 stands repealed.
- **January 2005:** The Board of Directors of IDBI Ltd., at its meeting held on January 20, 2005, approved the Scheme of Amalgamation, envisaging merging of IDBI Bank Ltd. with IDBI Ltd. Pursuant to the scheme approved by the Boards of both the banks, IDBI Ltd. will issue 100 equity shares for 142 equity shares held by shareholders in IDBI Bank Ltd. EGM has been convened on February 23, 2005 for seeking shareholder approval for the scheme

SIDBI

Small Industries Development Bank of India (SIDBI) was established in April 1990 as a wholly owned subsidiary of Industrial Development Bank of India (IDBI), under an Act of Indian Parliament to serve as the principal financial institution for promotion, financing and development of industry in the small scale sector and co-ordinating the functions of other institutions engaged in similar activities. As a result of an amendment to the SIDBI Act, SIDBI has since been made as an independent financial institution to cater to the wider range of SSI requirements.

SIDBI's Assistance to the small scale sector is channelised basically through 3 routes viz, Indirect Assistance, Direct

Assistance and Development and Support Services. SIDBI offers various schemes of assistance, designed to meet every need of small scale industries, under one roof. The unsecured bonds of SIDBI have been rated 'AAA' by leading domestic rating agencies viz. The Credit Rating Information Services of India Ltd. (CRISIL) and Credit Analysis and Research Ltd. (CARE). SIDBI is ranked 23rd in terms of Assets and 24th in terms of Capital among the top 50 Development Banks in the World *(Source: The Banker, London, June 2000)*. SIDBI is placing strong emphasis on technology development and absorption both for modernisation purposes and also for creating new enterprises and strengthening existing enterprises in high tech areas such as information technology.

SIDBI and Venture Capital Financing

SIDBI's Venture Capital Fund constituted in October 1992. It is utilised for direct investment in small scale units and contribution to Venture Capital Funds for onward lending to/ investment in small scale units. It has promoted 15 State/All India Level Venture Funds. 10 Funds are IT dedicated and the balance 5 are General Funds. Also promoted National level Fund NFSIT. SIDBI has so far made an aggregate commitment of Rs.1.5 billion (US$ 33.33 million), further, SIDBI has also taken the initiative in setting up of two Innovation and Incubation Centres in Indian Institute of Technology, Kanpur and Birla Institute of Technology, Mesra.

The objective of SIDBI's Venture Fund is to provide a window to entrepreneurs with ventures which have special characteristics to be innovative but at the same time may not qualify for assistance through the conventional route of term financing. SSI units involving new and untried processes and technologies which have scope for commercial application with characteristics of high risk and high return may be considered.

In turn, establishment of SIDBI Venture Capital Limited (SVCL) took place in July 1999 which is a wholly owned subsidiary of SIDBI, to act as an umbrella organisation to oversee the Venture Capital operation of SIDBI. SVCL will manage the various Venture Capital Funds launched/being launched by SIDBI.

SVCL Relationship

Besides financial assistance SVCL's role is to Help the entrepreneur to manage his business more effectively and achieve rapid growth in internationally competitive environment. Use SIDBI's close functional linkages with domestic and international venture capital funds/companies, Govt. agencies, financial institutions, commercial banks, foreign institutional investors, merchant bankers, consultancy agencies, management institutes, R&D organisations, software technology parks etc. to provide strategic support to assisted companies of this fund. Also to provide Indian Small enterprises not only with fund support but also information, market access, technology networking and hand holding required to add value to assisted units so as to enable them to become global companies and aim at future listing on the NASDAQ and other foreign stock exchanges

SIDBI, as the apex Financial Institution for the Small Scale Sector, has been playing a very active role in the evolution of Venture Capital financing in the country to support the risk capital requirements of the sector. SIDBI has been following a three tier approach in this regard. To this end, the Bank has been investing in several Venture Capital Funds for onward investments in the SME sector. These include several prominent funds such as India Leverage Fund, India Advantage Fund, India Development Fund. Recently SIDBI has partnered with Small Enterprise Assistance Fund, US and Kotak Mahindra Bank Ltd. in setting up India Growth Fund. Bank has also invested in a number of state level VC funds in collaboration with local institutions. The sanctions of the Bank relating to Venture Capital operations aggregate Rs. 450.36 crore through various routes, making it one of the largest VC players in the country.

SECTION II. PROFILES OF SELECTED BIOTECHNOLOGY COMPANIES IN ANDHRA PRADESH

Shantha Biotechnics Limited (SBL)

Shantha Biotechnics Limited (Shantha) is a pioneer in the biotechnology industry in India and was the first one to develop, manufacture and, market an indigenously developed Hepatitis-B Vaccine from r-DNA technology. Shantha is based in Hyderabad, India and was established in 1993. The first product launched commercially was SHANVACTM-B in 1997. Shantha's mission is to carry out research, development, manufacturing and distribution of genetically engineered human health care products, conforming to the highest International Standards, which would be cost effective and affordable to all sections of society. Shantha's Business Domain encompasses the complete spectrum of human health care biotechnology by adopting an integrated research, manufacturing and marketing model. Shantha is an R&D driven company and has ploughed back >25 per cent of its revenues till date into R&D activities.

Shantha is a 50:50 Joint Venture between Omani and Indian associates. It is headed by the Chairman, H.E. Yusuf Bin Alawi Abdullah of the Sultanate of Oman and the managing director Dr K I Varaprasad Reddy. The other Board of Directors of SBL are Mr. Khalil Ahmed, H.E. Ghassan, I. Shaker, Dr. T. Kodanda Rami Reddy and Mr. Subu M Kota. The Human Resources of SBL is 526, which comprises of R&D—98, Production—85, Engineering—44, QA and QC—55, Marketing and Sales—201 and Staff Functions—43.

In fact Shantha was started by Dr. K I Varaprasad Reddy, with the help of eminent scientists in 1993 forayed into the unexplored biotech arena in India. Their dedicated research led to the launch of SHANVACTM B, an r-DNA Hepatitis-B vaccine, India's first recombinant human healthcare product in 1997. SHANV ACTM_B is the First Indian Hepatitis-B vaccine pre-qualified by WHO-Geneva. Shantha has followed this success with launch of various Recombinant Biotherapeutic proteins. SHANFERONTM was launched in 2002 which is the first recombinant Human Interferon Alpha 2b expressed in the Yeast *Pichia pastoris* and is indicated in the treatment of Chronic Myeloid Leukemia; Renal Cell Carcinoma; Hepatitis-B; Hepatitis-C among other diseases.

SHANKINASETM was launched in October 2004 which is a recombinant Streptokinase, a life saving Drug used mainly in the indications of Acute Myocardial Infarction, Deep Vein Thrombosis and Pulmonary Embolism. SHANPOETINTM was launched in January 2005 which is a recombinant Human Erythropoietin expressed in CHO cells and produced in serum free media. SHANPOETINTM is indicated for treating anemia in chronic renal failure patients and anemia induced by Chemotherapy in cancer patients.

Plant: Facilities and Quality Systems

Shantha's manufacturing facility meets WHO cGMP standards. The following are the facilities at SBL:

- Aesthetically designed modern manufacturing facility with state-of-the-art computer controlled equipments
- WHO (Geneva) certification for Hepatitis B vaccine
- Modular in design with pre-fabricated materials
- Design and execution in consultation with GMP experts
- Conforming to the US FDA standards
- Supported with Engineering Services, Quality Control laboratory with modern analytical equipments and Animal House conforming to the Good Laboratory Practices (cGLP) Stores area conforming to the cGMP.

Also rigorous Quality Management programme as per ISO 9001 is practiced at Shantha. Analytical methods are validated as per ICH guidelines and testing is done on all batches of water, raw materials, in-process samples, finished products and packing material.

R&D Center and Plant

Shantha has a state of art R&D center spread over 40,000 sq ft., it is largest Biotech Research and Development Laboratory in India in private sector which includes an 8000 sq. ft. of class 10,000 area with world-class instruments and support facilities. Shantha's R&D efforts are mainly focused on Therapeutic products for Oncology and on vaccines. Shantha has developed Core Competence in the areas of Molecular Biology, Microbial Fermentation, Down stream process development for biologicals Protein Purification, Formulation and Lyophilization, Mammalian Cell Culture and Development of Monoclonal Antibodies.

Shantha also offers Contract R&D services such as cloning and expression of genes in various host systems, development and characterization of cell lines, fermentation and purification process development, large-scale production of proteins, and polyclonal/monoclonal antibodies against desired antigens.

Future Research areas of SBL

I. Vaccines:
- (1) Basic Pediatric Vaccines
- (2) Enhanced Pediatric Vaccines
- (3) Combination Vaccines
- (4) Adult and Travei Vaccines

II. Therapeutic Products
- (1) Tissues Plasminogen Activator
- (2) Anti GP IIb/IIIa
- (3) Human Insulin
- (4) Peg Interferon
- (5) TNF Alfa

III. Oncology Products:
- (1) G-CSF
- (2) Human Monoclonal Antibodies RM I, RM II, RM III, RM IV
- (3) EPO
- (4) Anti EGFR

IV. Diagnostic Kits:
(1) AFP ELISA
(2) Hepatitis B ELISA
(3) Hepatitis C ELISA
(4) HIV I+II ELISA

Marketing

Shantha has a well defined marketing setup which spans all of India and many parts of the World. The team comprises highly qualified Marketing and Sales Professionals with diverse experience and enjoys excellent relationship with more than 10000 Doctors, the Government, and over 600 Channel Partners and over 170 Sales Professionals cover the width and depth of the Country. Shantha caters to major international markets including Asia-Pacific, Africa, CIS and Latin America in addition to supplies to Global Organizations like UNICEF and PAHO. Shantha has built up a strong network of Business Partners in many key markets and is currently exporting its products to more than 40 countries around the world.

BioServe Biotechnologies India Pvt. Ltd.

BioServe Biotechnologies India Pvt. Ltd., located in Hyderabad, A.P. India, specializes in providing custom laboratory services, genetic research and the development of diagnostic reagents. It has been deep rooted in the Indian scientific community since 1994 through Rama Biotechnologies and now with the introduction of BioServe-India, it plans to offer the services first hand from its newly established laboratory facilities. The goal of the company is to provide the Indian research community access to the newest and most essential technology enabling the practice of the highest levels of research and development in today's rapidly progressing intemational biotechnology market.

Company's foundation is based upon the successful, long standing business model and philosophy of BioServe Biotechnologies USA Ltd. under which guidance and direction the company will flourish as BioServe USA has sufficient long standing experience in this industry to guide and direct the emerging Indian research population, since 1989.

BioServe India will build upon this philosophy by assembling an exceptional team of experienced and dedicated professionals. Its blend of molecular biology specialists, laboratory technicians and support personnel enables Bioserve to meet the most challenging and complex customer requirements in the areas of DNA synthesis, DNA sequencing and genotyping/SNP analysis.

BioServe India maintains the highest level of quality control analysis for every service and product involved in our production. The quality of BioServe Oligonucleotides and other molecular biology services have been validated by academic institutions, clinical research laboratories, diagnostic service organizations, biotechnology companies, private research firms, amongst others. Research and Development are an integral part of the company's effort to improve its products and expand services. Currently, the company offer Oligonucleotide synthesis, DNA sequencing and DNA extraction services. Hence the plans of BioServe in the immediate future include the implementation of genomics bases services including high throughput genotyping. Hence the total capital investment made by the company, project cost and the key financial indicators of the company over a period of five years can be seen from the Tables 6.6, 6.7 and 6.8.

Bharat Biotech International Limited

Bharat Biotech International Limited, Hyderabad city based Pharmaceutical giant, has the second largest biotech plant facility in the world with a capacity to produce over 100 million doses of Hepatitis B vaccine. It is the first company in the world to perfect a technology that permits recovery of the Hepatitis B protein without the use of heavy metals and is also the First Biotech company awarded with two collaborative research grants from the Department of Science and Technology, Govt. of India.

Table 6.6: Total capital invested along promoters participation

Particulars	*2000-01 Rs.(in Lakhs)*	*2001-02 Rs.(in Lakhs)*	*2002-03 Rs.(in Lakhs)*	*2003-04 Rs.(in Lakhs)*	*2004-05 Rs.(in Lakhs)*
Total Capital	3.09	3.09	3.09	3.09	3.09
1. Equity					
—Promoters					
—Venture Capitalist's Share					
—Others					
2. Loans					
—Banks					
—FIs					
—VCOs					
—Others					

Source: Primary Data

Table 6.7: Project Costs and Financial Means

Particulars	*Expenditure Incurred (Rs. In Lakhs)*
Land and Site Development (Rs.)	
Building and Civil Works (Rs.)	—
Plant and Machinery (Imported) (Rs.)	—
Plant Machinery (indigenous) (Rs.)	82.00
Erection and Commissioning (Rs.)	10.36
Miscellaneous Fixed Assets (Rs.)	—
Operating Expenses (incl. Advances) (Rs.)	20.85
Prelim and Preop Expenses (Rs.)	1.09
Marketing Expenses (Rs.)	—
Contingencies (Rs.)	0.81
Interest during Development Period (Rs.)	—
Margin Money for Working Capital (Rs.)	—

Source: Primary Data

Table 6.8: Important Financial Indicators (Rs. In Lakhs)

Parameters	*2000-01*	*2001-02*	*2002-03*	*2003-04*	*2004-05*
Total Income (Rs.Lakhs)	10.31	N.A.	8.62	68.18	N.A.
Materials/Income (%)	28.41	N.A.	27.53	31.20	N.A.
Interest/Income (%)	N.A.	N.A.	10%	9.37	N.A

The person heading this unique company is Dr. Krishna Ella, Ph.D. from The University of Wisconsin, Madison and a M.S.,from The University of Hawaii. Dr.Krishna Ella has also won a lot of Academic Awards such as the National Research Service Award, Rotary Foundation (Chicago, Illinois) Fellowship, Indian Council of Agri. Research Fellow, University Gold Medallist for highest C.G.P.A., American Spring (ASPEE) Gold Medallist and also bagged the Rotary International prize. He has also been honoured with the 'Dr. K.C. Chatterjee Memorial Award' from the Indian Pharamaceutical Association, India in 1999. He had been the Member, National Task Force, Industrial Biotechnology in 1999. He was also the: Vice-President, All India Biotech Association, India (1999-2000). Presently, he is the Member-Pharma Task Force, Govt. of A.P.

The company has taken up the challenge of providing premier health care products to the common man and also taken the route of Genetic Engineering and Biotechnology to achieve the goal of ensuring a healthy tomorrow. It was established in the year 1996, the company is a torch bearer in the field of developing Next-Generation Vaccines and Biopharmaceuticals through original and collaborative research. Its pioneering and incessant research led to the launch of Revac-B, the immensely effective Recombinant Vaccine for Hepatitis-B, the killer disease, in 1998. It is the world's second largest Hepatits B manufacturing plant with a capacity of 100 million doses per annum, conforming to USFDA, UK-MCA and WHO standards.

Its major Product is REVAC - B which is Second-generation genetically engineered vaccine developed in recombinant strains of yeast, indicated for vaccination against Hepatitis B. The Worlds first Cesium Chloride free (CsCl)

Vaccine manufactured using the patented innovative in-house production process - HIMAX Technology.

Bharat Biotech has also became the first Biotechnology company in the country and second of its kind in the world to manufacture and market Recombinant Streptokinase the primary drug for dissolving blood clots, a common occurrence during a heart attack. The Drug Controller General of India, the national regulatory authority for Indian pharmacopoeia, granted the commercial licence to BBIL on Thursday, August 14, 2003.

The company has bagged the National Award for Promotion of Biotechnology in the area of Medical Biotechnology- Vaccines and also bagged the National Award For Best R & D Efforts in Industry. Hence the total capital investment made by the company, project cost and the key financial indicators of the company over a period of five years can be seen from the following tables.

Table 6.9: Total Capital Invested along with your participation/share

Particulars	*2000-01* Rs.(in Lakhs)	*2001-02* Rs.(in Lakhs)	*2002-03* Rs.(in Lakhs)	*2003-04* Rs.(in Lakhs)	*2004-05* Rs.(in Lakhs)
Total Capital	921.06	940.90	960.90	960.90	1155.90
1. Equity					
—Promoters	628.99	648.83	648.83	648.83	843.83
—Venture Capitalist's Share	200.00	200.00	200.00	200.00	200.00
—Others	92.07	92.07	92.07	92.07	92.07
2. Loans	228	465	254	114	0
—Banks	192.50	214	700	645	1130
—FIs	1195	122.50	50	0	0
—VCOs		1175	1065	1000	918
—Others					

Source: Primary Data

Table 6.10: Project Costs and Financial Means

Particulars	*Expenditure Incurred (Rs. In Lakhs)*
Land and Site Development (Rs.)	20
Building and Civil Works (Rs.)	85
Plant and Machinery (Imported) (Rs.)	638
Plant Machinery (indigenous) (Rs.)	100
Erection and Commissioning (Rs.)	
Miscellaneous Fixed Assets (Rs.)	85
Operating Expenses (incl. Advances) (Rs.)	184
Prelim and Preop Expenses (Rs.)	2
Marketing Expenses (Rs.)	
Contingencies (Rs.)	39
Interest during Development Period (Rs.)	
Margin Money for Working Capital (Rs.)	68
Total	**1221**

Source: Primary Data

Table 6.11: Important Financial Indicators (Rs. In Lakhs)

Parameters	*2000-01*	*2001-02*	*2002-03*	*2003-04*	*2004-05*
Total Income (Rs.Lakhs)	2346.66	2738.29	2620.18	3446.19	4037.27
Materials/Income (%)	6.32	4.97	1.2	33.3	34.9
Interest/Income (%)	5.92	7.33	7.56	4.23	2.32
Net Profit/Income (%)	23.87	16.6	10.08	10.2	10.76
Operating BEP (%)					
Project IRR (%)	30	302	30	30	30
EPS (Rs.)	4.74	4.83	2.75	3.65	3.75
Return on Equity (%)					

Source: Primary Data

Dr. Reddy's Laboratories

Dr. Reddy's Laboratories was founded by Dr. Anji Reddy, a entrepreneur-scientist, in 1984. The DNA of the company is drawn from its founder and his vision to establish India's first discovery led global pharmaceutical company. In fact, it is this spirit of entrepreneurship that has shaped the company to become what it is today.

Dr. Anji Reddy, having moved out of Standard Organics Limited, a company he had successfully co-founded, started Dr. Reddy's Laboratories with $ 40,000 in cash and $120,000 in bank loan! Today, the company with revenues of Rs.1947 crore (US $446 million), as of fiscal year 2005, is India's second largest pharmaceutical company and the youngest among its peer group.

The company has several distinctions to its credit. Being the first pharmaceutical company from Asia Pacific (outside Japan) to be listed on the New York Stock Exchange (NYSE) (on April 11, 2001). As always, Dr. Reddy's chose to do anything in the most difficult circumstances against widespread skepticism, coming up trumps, its stock as oversubscribed and became the best performing IPO.

Dr. Anji Reddy is well known for his passion for research and drug discovery. Dr. Reddy's started its drug discovery programme in 1993 and within three years it achieved its first breakthrough by outlicensing an anti-diabetes molecule to Novo Nordisk in March 1997. With this very small but significant step, the Indian industry went through a paradigm shift in its image from being known as just 'copycats' to 'innovators', hence, through its success, Dr. Reddy's pioneered drug discovery in India. There are several such inflection points in the company's evolution from a bulk drug (API) manufacturer into a vertically integrated global pharmaceutical company today.

Today, the company manufactures and markets API (Bulk Actives), Finished Dosages and Biologics in over 100 countries worldwide, in addition to having a very promising Drug Discovery Pipeline. When Dr. Reddy's started its first big move in 1986 from manufacturing and marketing bulk actives to the domestic (Indian) market to manufacturing and exporting difficult-to-manufacture bulk actives such as Methyldopa to highly regulated overseas markets, it had to not only overcome regulatory and legal hurdles but also battle deeply entrenched mind-set issues of Indian Pharma being seen as producers of 'cheap' and therefore 'low quality' pharmaceuticals. Today, the Indian pharma industry, in stark contrast, is known globally for its proven high quality-low cost advantage in delivering safe and effective pharmaceuticals.

In fact, Dr. Reddy's was able to establish itself as a supplier of high quality pharmaceuticals very early on in the global market. An interesting anecdote illustrates this succinctly. The company's process for Ibuprofen, a popular anti-inflammatory drug, was so advanced that Ethyl Corporation, US, had to accept its superiority in front of the US Trade Representative and ask for tariffs to be put against Dr. Reddy's to achieve a level playing field. Today, Dr. Reddy's continues its journey by leveraging on its 'Low Cost, High Intellect' advantage and Foraying into new markets and new businesses. Taking on new challenges and growing stronger and more capable. Each failure and each success renewing the sense of purpose and helping the company evolve.

With over 950 scientists working across the globe, around the clock, the company continues its relentless march forward to discover and deliver a breakthrough medicine to address an unmet medical need and make a difference to people's lives worldwide. And when it does that, it would only be the beginning and yet it would be the most important step. As Lao Tzu wrote a long time ago, 'Even a 1000 mile journey starts with a single step.

Genotex International India Pvt.

Genotex International India Pvt. Ltd. is a privately held company and is extensively involved in R&D of various specialized biotechnology products such as Molecular biologicals, Taq DNA Polymerase, T., Polynucleotide Kinase, T., DNA ligase, Molecular Weight Markers, etc., Peptides and Aloe vera products such as Aloe vera gel in different concentrations, Aloe vera powder (spray dried, freeze dried), Aloin of different grades of purity etc. The company is located at S.P.Biotech Park, Turkapally, near Hyderabad with R&D and production facility. It has Aloe vera crop, grown organically in about 100 acres fann, without using chemical pesticides and fertilizers. The Aloe crop is of three years old.

The Genotex has a Scientific Advisory Board (SAB). The members of the Advisory Board are attached to Premier Universities and Research organizations of the world. The members of advisory board are:

(1) Dr. C.R. Bhatia is a former secretary Department of Biotechnology,
(2) Prof. Jeffrey L. Bennetzen, Ph. D is a professor at the Purdue University, USA,
(3) Dr. Swapan Datta, Ph.D., has been associated with the group that invented Golden Rice,
(4) Prof. Dr. Andy Periera, Ph.D., an internationally acclaimed scientist, leading a strong group in plant biotechnology and genomics research at Plant Research International, Netherlands,
(5) Dr. C.V.Rao, Ph. D., is the Associate Chief, Division of Nutrionational Carcinogenesis and Head of Chemoprevention program at American Health Foundation, Valhalla, New York, and
(6) Prof. Dr. Heinz Saedler, Ph.D., Director Max Planck Institute, Plant Molecular Genetics, Koln, Germany.

Key Management Personnel

The management of Genotex is a well-balanced team of talented experts in select faculties of biotechnology and project management. Together they form an immense collective talent pool, which will manage this project. They are:

Mr. C. Devender Reddy, Director

Mr. C.D. Reddy is a former Bank executive with vast experience in money management. After voluntary retirement 10 years ago, he has set up seed production industry and plantation units. He has been a progressive farmer and well versed with modern agricultural practices.

Dr. Arjula R. Reddy, Director

Arjula Reddy is a scientist in Department of Plant Sciences in the University of Hyderabad. His research area includes Biotechnology, Genomics and Applied Genetics. He has done his M.Sc. in Genetics (specialization in genetics and plant breeding) from Osmania University and also holds a Ph.D. degree in genetics. He has established Genomics facility at University of Hyderabad and sequenced 1000s of genes. He has also helped in generating transgenic plants carrying genes from other sources and evaluated them.

Dr. Jesse Jaynes, Director

Jesse Jaynes is the Chairman and President of the Nova Tero Foundation. He holds a bachelor's degree in Zoology and has also done Ph.D. in Biochemistry. He started his career as a tutor in Maths, Chemistry and Statistics in Southern Utah College, Cedar City, Utah. Before joining Nova Tero foundation, he was working as the Chief Scientist of Demegen, Inc, Pittsburgh. There are number of US patents which have been granted to him on microorganisms and peptides for the control and prevention of various diseases. Along with the various books and publications of his own he has membership in various scientific societies.

Mr. G. Seenayya, Director

G. Seenayya is a Professor of Microbiology (Retd.) in Osmania University, Hyderabad. His field of specialization is in Anaerobic Fermentations and Environmental and Applied Microbiology. He has a teaching experience of 20 years in General Microbiology and Food and Agricultural Microbiology. He has helped the institute in establishing of laboratory for Anaerobic Fermentations and also has successfully completed a number of research projects. He holds two patents one on aspartame production and another one on enzymes.

Mrs. A. Vaishali, M.S., USA, Director

Mrs.Vaishali is a post graduate in Genetics and later in Medical Sciences and a practicing assistant now at Neurology Division in Le High Valley Hospital in Pennsylvania, USA. She has experience in molecular analysis, fungal genetics, and human diseases.

Mr. Vamsee Chintalapani, B.Tech (Computer Sciences), Director

Mr. Vamsee is a graduate in computer science and presently a manager of a consultants firm in New Jersey, USA. Over a period of three years, he is well versed in the fields of human resources management and software management.

Mission

The mission of Genotex is to do business through products that improve human and animal health care. Enhance the resistance and nutritional value of plants, and develop advanced research tools and proprietary process for production of therapeutics and other proteins in plant expression systems.

Genotex has organically I grown Aloe Vera crop and manufactures gel, I juice, cream, powder, ~ and aloin up to 95 per cent purity using clean and green technologies. Genotex is developing novel technologies using Aloe Vera gel as a base for drug delivery through topical applications. Genotex has acquired and developed technologies and products including enzymes and molecular biologicals used extensively in biotechnology research, development, diagnosis and production. Genotex is also venturing into production of recombinant therapeutic molecules for human and animal health.

Genotex is embarking on developing next generation technologies using plant systems as bioreactors for production of target molecules. Genotex will take up contract research and services including design, synthesis and validation of novel therapeutic molecules and industrial enzymes.

Product Profile

1. Aloe Vera

Genotex maintains optimized sanitary conditions for processing Aloe Vera leaves grown organically in well-organized farms. Genotex takes minimal acceptable time between harvesting and primary processing.

2. Formulations from Aloe Vera

Aloe Vera juice I gel (Geno Aloe gel) for oral consumption 100 per cent pure, to improve immunity, cure and prevent intestinal ailments and as a nutritional supplement Geno Aloe gel creams:

Rejuvenating cream: To rejuvenating the skin to remove under eye Blackness, etc.

Moisturizing cream: To maintain the natural moisture balance of the facial skin for pimples, scars etc.

Wounds and burns cream: For curing wounds and burns, injuries without even making a scar etc. Geno Aloe.

3. Shampoo

Cleanse hair, moisturize, soothe and heal scalp, and help in controlling dandruff, scalp dermatitis and psoriasis.

4. Geno Aloe Shaving Gel

Gives a closer, smoother and gentler shave. Soothing aloe in this gel will protect and moisturize your skin. The added Menthol will give you a 'super cooled feel'.

5. Geno Aloe Face Wash and Body Wash

The cleansing, moisturizing and conditioning properties of aloe vera kills bacteria and germs on contact while it soothes, heals and re-moisturizes skin.

6. Geno Aloe Galvanic Lotion

The Aloe present in it is believed to penetrate the skin all the way to the muscle layer and imparts healthy and moisturizing benefits into the very deepest layers of the skin, something oil, oil-water based products cannot do. The enzyme in aloe vera exfoliates dead cells, rejuvenates skin cells and generates healthy new cells much faster than normal cell reproduction. On regular and constant use, the skin looks younger and healthier.

Enzymes and Molecular biologicals:

Product	*Package Size*
100 bp DNA ladder	50 J.1g (for 100 applications) 100 J.1g (for 200 applications)
500 bp DNA ladder	50 J.19 (for 100 applications) 100 J.1g (for 200 applications)
200 bp DNA ladder	50 J.19 (for 100 applications) 100 J.1g (for 200 applications)
100 bp+500 bp DNA ladder	50 J.1g (for 100 applications) 100 J.1g (for 200 applications)
Protein Molecular Weight Marker	0.5 ml (for 100 mini gel applications) 1 ml (for 200 mini gel applications)
GenoTaq (Recombinant Taq DNA Polymerase)	250 Units, 500 Units, 1000 Units
T 4 Polynucleotide Kinase	500 Units, 1000 Units
T4 DNA Ligase	20,000 Units, 100,000 Units
T 4 RNA Ligase	500 Units, 1000 Units
T/A cloning system for PCR Product Cloning:	10 reactions, 30 reactions

Peptides for the treatment of various diseases (Genopep).

The Genotex has obtained patented peptides for the treatment of infected bums and wounds, prevention of sexually transmitted infections (8118), including AID8 and in the treatment of Cancer. The proprietary processes are in the initial stages of execution.

Genetically Engineered Rice

The Genotex intends to develop genetically engineered rice that carries a designed protein that confer disease resistance to plants and have enhanced nutritional value. The proprietary processes for the production of therapeutics and proteins in plant expression systems are in the initial stages of execution.

As it has stated in its mission, earlier that it wanted to improve the health care of human and animal alike, so it feels that serving its customer with superior quality products will be the first step in the that direction. The company ensures that all its products are made from finest raw materials under the supervision of experienced professionals.

Infrastructure

The company has state-of-the art production unit with sophisticated machines. It has a team of highly experienced staff with decades of experience in their respective fields. The research and development department professionals are toiling round the clock to come up with some highly developed products. Genotex has a competent team of qualified scientists to carry out its activities. The team has experts in the fields of molecular biology, biotechnology, microbiology, plant genetic engineering, biochemistry and medicine. Highly distinguished scientific advisors and consultants back Genotex. So, Genotex experts have pioneered large-scale Aloe Vera culture in organized farms and bulk processing.

7

Perceptional Analysis of Selected Biotech Companies

The success of Biotech undertakings depends not only on investee's effort but also on Venture Capital investor's contribution, because VCCs financing system, and as a partner venture capital investor play a key role in deciding the fate of undertakings. So, in the present chapter an attempt is made to analyze the perception of biotech companies over the role of venture capital in development and promotion of biotechnology through the primary data collected with the help of a questionnaire administered to the selected venture capital undertakings of A.P.I.D.C—Venture Capital Limited, IDBI Venture Limited, ICICI and others at Hyderabad.

Investees' Understanding about Venture Capital

Venture Capital is not an old concept, it is quite different to traditional financing, because the venture capitalist interferes in the investees business as partner unlike in traditional type of financing system. So the entrepreneurs need a complete awareness on venture capital. The data collected in this regard is analyzed and shown in Table 7.1 explains about the understanding of undertaking firms on venture capital concept.

It is evident from table that there is a different perception over Venture Capital in the minds of the entrepreneurs. Fifty per cent of respondents opined that VC is the capital investment for only high-tech projects. Whereas, others opined that Venture Capital is capital investment for unexploited ideas and innovative projects at equal proportion. Hence, it is understood that VC is the capital investment in an enterprise which carries high element of risk and uncertainty as well as new and innovative technologies that can yield higher returns.

Table 7.1: Investees understanding on Venture Capital

	Understanding	*Respondents*	%
1	Risk Capital	0	0
2	Capital investment for only high tech projects	2	50
3	Capital investment for unexploited ideas	1	25
4	Capital investment for innovative projects	1	25
	Total	4	100

Source: Primary Data

Sources of Investees Awareness on Venture Capital

There are many ways of sources to aware about venture capital such as corporate news, venture capital fund organizations, experience of beneficiaries etc. In Tables 7.2 and 7.3, the source of investors awareness on venture capital in general and Company through which they got finance particular is shown.

Table 7.2: Investees Awareness on Sources of VC

	Awareness through	*Respondents*	%
1	Corporate News and Journals	2	40
2	Venture Capital Fund Organizations		0
3	Financial Analysts, Advisors and Consultants	2	40
4	Developmental Financial Institutions		0
5	Personal Awareness	1	20
	Total	5	100

Table 7.3: Sources of Investees Awareness on VCCs

	Awareness through	*Respondents*	%
1	Corporate News and Journals	1	20
2	Beneficiaries	1	20
3	Financial Analysts, Advisors and Consultants	3	60
4	Developmental Financial Institutions		0
5	Personal Awareness		0
	Total	5	100

Source: Primary Data

It can be seen from Tables 7.2 and 7.3, that investee's awareness on sources of Venture Capital. Majority of respondents got awareness about availability of Venture Capital through Corporate News and Journals (40%) and Financial Analysts, Advisors and Consultants (40%). Whereas, the rest of the respondents got awareness through their own perception and personal knowledge (20%). Hence, the Corporate News, Journals and Financial Advisors are the main source of awareness over Venture Capital. As far as source of investees awareness on Venture Capital companies from which they got finance is concerned, it is somewhat different because beneficiaries (20%) of various venture capital funds influenced a lot in making awareness to the potential entrepreneurs on Venture Capital activity. However, in this regard the role of corporate news and journals (20%) is at par with beneficiaries' role. It can be also seen from the table that significant role of financial analysts, advisors and consultants as source of awareness (60%). It indicates that financial analysts, advisors and consultants are playing a dominant role in making potential entrepreneurs of biotechnology to aware about Venture Capital availability and the priorities of the funds operating in India.

Investees Approach to Venture Capital Companies

The entrepreneurs when they want to get venture finance they need to approach the Venture Capital companies/funds either personally, or through financial advisers or in any other way. Table 7.4., shows how the selected investees approached various to get venture finance venture capital companies/funds.

Table 7.4: Investees approach to VCC

Approach VCC		*Respondents*	*%*
1	Personally	1	20
2	Through Financial Analysts, Advisors and Consultants	4	80
3	Other VCs		0
	Total	5	100

Source: Primary Data

It is apparent from Table 7.4 that the investee's approach to Venture Capital Companies. Majority of the respondents (80%) approached the Venture Capital Companies through Financial Analysts, Advisors and Consultants. Whereas, the others (20%) approached Venture Capital Companies personally to get finance. It is indicated by the analysis very clearly that even in getting Venture Finance, Financial Analysts, Advisors and Consultants are playing very crucial role.

Critical Factors of Selection

Venture Capital Companies generally base upon certain critical factors for selection of any proposal for extending their venture finance. Here in this regard the critical factors that were made them to select the projects of the respondent companies are analyzed in Table 7.5.

Table 7. 5: Critical factors of Project Selection by VCC

Factors		*Respondents*	*%*
1	Various services under one roof (very uncommon in India)	1	20
2	Technological capabilities and viability of the product	3	60
3	Feasibility and past record of the company	1	20
	Total	5	100

Source: Primary Data

Table 7.5 reveals that the critical factors for selection of respondents units by various Venture Capital Companies/ Funds they are: (1) Technological capabilities and viability of the project (60%), (2) Feasibility and past record of the company (20%) and (3) Various services under one roof which is very uncommon in India (20%). However, the major factor that influences the selection criterion is technology capabilities.

Stage-wise Finance

Unlike traditional financial institutions, a venture capital fund provides the finance to undertakings at different stages. Data collected pertaining to the same from different companies selected for the study is analysed and shown in Table 7.6 .

Table 7.6: Details of finance Extended by VCC at stages (Rs. In Lakhs)

	Company	*Early Stage*	*Expansion*	*Acquisition*
1	BioServe	300	—	—
2	Bharat Biotech	220	—	—
3	Shanta*	—	—	—
4	Genotex Intl India Ltd*	—	—	—
5	KCP Biotech*	—	—	—
6	Dr. Reddy's*	—	—	—

* Companies in process to take-up the early stage finance.
Source: Primary Data

It is evident from the table that except two companies (BioServe and Bharat Biotech), others are in process to take-up the early stage finance.

Difficulties in Getting Venture Finance

As venture capital is at take-off in India, still there are certain problems with which it is suffering a lot. So the difficulties that were experienced by the respondent companies are analyzed and shown in Table 7.7.

Table 7.7 clearly explains that the difficulties one can face in getting Venture Capital finance. According to the respondents experience, it is understood that the major difficulties are: (1) Making Venture Capital Companies to trust the new entrepreneurs, (2) Problems faced by VCC with similar type of investments which becomes an hindrance to entrepreneurs, (3) Higher interest rates, (4) Delay in sanction of funds, (5) Collateral Security, and (6) Looking for returns without any gestation period.

Table 7.7: Difficulties in getting finance

	Bio-Serve		*Bharat Biotech*		*Shanta*		*Genotex Intl India Ltd*		*KCP Biotech*		*Dr. Reddys*	
Difficulties faced	*Yes*	*No*	*Yes*	*No*	*Yes*	*No*	*Yes*	*No*	*Yes*	*No*	*Yes*	*No*
1 Trust in new entrepreneurs			√									
2 Problems faced by them in similar investment			√									
3 Higher interest rates			√									
4 Delay in sanction			√									
5 Collateral security							√					
6 Looking for returns without any gestation period							√					

Source: Primary Data

How Commercial was Venture Capital

Commercial aspect of venture capital is not so high as it promotes the new and innovative ideas at initial stages and helps the economy a lot by promoting the budding entrepreneurs having good and sound knowledge in technology and enterprise skills. Data collected on the opinions of the selected companies of the same is analyzed and shown in Table 7.8.

Table 7.8: How commercial was VC

		Respondents	*%*
1	Very high	2	40
2	Average	3	60
3	Not commercial		0
	Total	5	100

Source: Primary Data

Essential Qualities that VCs Look in Entrepreneurs

When respondents were asked about the commerciality of VC, most of them (60%) opined that it is average and rest of them opined it as very high (40%).

To extend the finance and undertake the projects of entrepreneuring, VCCs look for different qualities. Table 7.9 analyses the same with selected biotech under takings.

Table 7.9: Qualities VC look in Entrepreneurs

	Qualities	*No of Respondents*	
		Yes	*No*
1	Commitment, truthfulness, capitation to convert ideas into reality	5	—
2	Idea, feasibility and return on investment	5	—
3	New developmental works which can lead to patents	5	—
4	Technology and previous background	5	—

Source: Primary Data

It is evident from Table 7.9 that the qualities required for Venture Capital finance in entrepreneurs. It is found that the most essential qualities are: (1) Commitment, truthfulness, capitation to convert ideas into reality, (2) Idea, feasibility and return on investment, (3) New developmental works which can lead to patents, and (4) Technology and previous background.

Competitors

In biotechnology industry the competition is very intensive and increasing day-by-day, it is due to increasing importance of the sector itself and flow of global funds into the sector. Data collected in this regard is analyzed and presented in the following Table 7.10.

Table 7.10: Competitors

	Name of the Company	*Potential market for the product*	*Name of the competitors*	
			Domestic	*Overseas*
1	BioServe	D and O	Bangalore Genei *Sigma Group*	Microsynt Organics
2	Bharat Biotech	D and O	GSK Serum Institute	Wruchardt, LG Life Sciences
3	Shanta	D and O	GSK, Roche, Bharat Biotech, Serum Institute	Wruchardt, Jhonson and Jhonson
4	Genotex Intl India Ltd	D and O	Both domestic and overseas market	
5	KCP Biotech	D and O	Overseas market	
6	Dr. Reddys	D and O	DO	

D—Domestic and O—Overseas
Source: Primary Data

It can be seen from Table 10 that the competitors of selected Biotech company both in domestic and overseas market. Particularly in domestic market, the competitors are Bangalore Genei Sigma Group, GSK Serum Institute, Roche, Bharat Biotech. On the other hand the competitors in the overseas market are Microsynt Organics, Wruchardt, LG Life Sciences and Jhonson and Jhonson.

Investees' Opinion on Performance of their Venture

Venture Capital undertakings normally take 5 to 8 years to come out with success. So investees need to monitor and appraise the performance of their ventures time to time. Data collected in this regards is analysed and presented in Table 7.11.

Table 7.11: Investees opinion on performance of their venture

		No.of Respondents	*%*
1	Satisfactory	3	60
2	Not Satisfactory	2	40
	Total	5	100

Source: Primary Data

Table 7.11 reveals that the opinion of respondents over the performance of their ventures. It is very clear that 60 per cent of respondents are very confident and have absolute satisfaction over their ventures' performance. On the other hand, others felt that as their ventures are at an early stage, it is not possible to adjudge the performance.

Investees' Opinion on the Role of VCC Financed their Projects

Investees' opinion on the role of various venture capital funds from which they got the finance is shown in Table 7.12.

Table 7.12: Investees opinion on the role of VCC financed their projects

	Opinion	*Respondents*	%
1	Good	1	20
2	Satisfactory	3	60
3	Poor	1	20
4	Cant' say	0	0
	Total	5	100

Source: Primary Data

When respondents were asked about their opinion over the role of VCC financed their projects, most of them (60%) felt that it is satisfactory and rest of them have given mixed opinion as good and poor (20% each).

Management Style of the VCC

Venture Capital is quite different to traditional type of finance, so the management style of venture capitalist should be very distinguishable for ultimate success of undertakings. The analysis pertaining to the same is made in the Table 7.13.

Table 7.13: Management style of the VCC

		No. of Respondents	%
1	Encouraging	1	25
2	Leading by interaction	1	25
3	Strategic partner	2	50
	Total	4	100

Source: Primary Data

It is evident from Table 7.13 that the management style of various VCCs through the experience of the respondents. The management styles that were exhibited by Venture Capital Companies/funds are: (1) Encouraging, (2) Leading by interaction, and (3) Strategic partner. It explains that the management style of VCCs differs from company to company which is a critical factor of success of any Venture Capital fund.

Opinion on Additional Services from VCCs

Besides investing money, venture capitalist can also render different types of services for the benefit of the undertakings. Data collected in this regard is critically analyses and presented in Table 7.14.

Table 7.14: Opinion on additional services of VCCs

	Opinion on additional Services of VCC		%
1	Marketing and Strategic Services	1	20
2	Moral support and building the corporate image through existing clientele	1	20
3	Arranging meetings and giving an approach to meet the Govt. Officials.	1	20
4	Not relevant	2	40
	Total	5	100

Source: Primary Data

When respondents were asked about their opinion on additional services provided by VCCs besides investing money, they revealed that they could get Marketing and Strategic Services. Moral support in building the corporate image through existing clientele and arranging meetings and giving an approach to meet the Govt. Officials as additional services. Hence, 40 per cent of respondents denied the provision of additional services as they are at budding stage.

Association with VCCs

Generally a cordial relationship will take place between venture capital investor and investee because the nature of venture capital. So Venture Capital investee may try to continue relationship with the investor till to get success. So the data pertaining to same is analyzed and presented to understand the preferences of the selected investees as far as time period is concerned to continue with their VCCs in Table 7.15.

Table.7.15: Association with VCCs

	Year	*Respcndents*	%
1	1—5 Years	3	75
2	5—10 years		
3	Above 10 years		
4	Forever		
5	Depends upon the experience	1	25
	Total	4	100

Source: Primary Data

It is evident from Table 7.15 that most of the Biotech undertakings (75%) are willing to continue their association with VCCs, 1 to 5 years time period maximum as VCs maintain a positive relationship and willing to support R&D on continuous basis. On the other hand 25 per cent of companies were not in a position to respond as it was first approach for them towards such type of investment.

Ranking of VCCs

Based on the responses of the selected companies the performance of venture capital companies as a whole is adjudged in terms of qualitative rankings as very good, good and satisfactory. Analysis of the same is shown in Table 7.16.

Table 7.16: Ranking of VCCs

	Ranking	*Respondents*	%
1	Very Good	1	20
2	Good	3	60
3	Satisfactory	1	20
	Total	5	100

Source: Primary Data

Table 7.16 reveals the ranking of VCCs according to opinions of respondents. 60 per cent of respondents opined that VCCs are good, whereas others have ranked them as very good and satisfactory (20 % each). Hence, opinions of respondents reveal that they got good experience with VCCs.

VCC Role-Proactive or Interfering

As we discussed earlier in one table that the role of venture capitalist should be very proactive in making the undertakings achieve the goals enunciated. Data related to same is analysed and shown in Table 7.17.

Table 7.17: VCC role—Proactive or Interfering

	Role	*Respondents*	%
1	Proactive	5	100
2	Interfering	0	0
	Total	5	100

Source: Primary Data

Table 7.17 is evident for the role of VCCs in development and promotion of biotech ventures through proactive nature. All selected undertakings opined that the Venture Capital Companies from which they got money for their ventures have played very proactive role in providing money as well as rendering other services. Hence, it is evident that as the success of VC depends on the role play of the Venture Capitalist, VCCs have played such role to see the success and for the reasons of (1) VCC act not only supports the entrepreneur with need based financial assistance in high tech projects and the interference is minimal, (2) Risk taking to become globally viable, (3) Leveraging in-house capabilities, (4) To get the results desired in terms of finance, and (5) Find suitable partners in the market.

Attitude of VCCs

Attitude of Venture Capital Companies is distinguishable to traditional type of finance. Data collected regarding the same is analyzed and shown in Table 7.18.

Table 7.18: Respondents opinion on the attitude of VCCs

Type of attitude	*Respondents*	%
Good as a Partner	5	100
Owner	0	0
Total	5	100

Source: Primary Data

When respondents were asked about their opinion on the attitude of VCCs, they felt that the attitude of VCCs is good as a partner and they never find the owner attitude with their VCCs.

Free Services Provided by VCC

Generally Venture Capital Companies provides free services at the most, but here through the data we got a different experience as the analysis shows that majority of the respondents denies the same. Data is collected and analyzed in this regard is shown very clearly in Table 7.19.

Table 7.19: Free services provided by VCC

		Respondents	%
1	Yes	2	40
2	No	3	60
	Total	5	100

Source: Primary Data

Table 7.19 reveals that 40 per cent of respondent companies have enjoyed so many services from their VCCs for which they would not have paid anything. Whereas, 60 per cent of respondents have paid for such services. Hence, it is clear that VCCs are not providing managerial and other services for free of cost, because, they are actively involved in the whole process of the undertakings for which they collect managerial fee.

Venture Capital (VC) A Boon for New Biotechnology and Economic Development

Venture Capital is a new and innovative financial service emerged to cater to the needs of the technocrats and scientists having novel ideas that can help the economy a lot to leap into development state. So it can be asserted that venture capital is a boon for biotechnology and economic development of any nation. Data collected in this regard is analyzed and shown in Table 7. 20.

Table 7. 20: Venture Capital a Boon for New Biotechnology and Economic Development

	Opinion	*No. of Respondents*	%
1	Yes	5	100
2	No	0	0
	Total	5	100

Source: Primary Data

Table 7.20 reveals the opinions of respondent companies on VC as a boon for biotechnology and economic development of a nation. All most of all the companies opined that Venture Capital Contribution is very significant for the economic development as it willing to fund for fresh and innovative ideas and suitable financial instrument for exploiting the new and innovative Bio-technologies as they are risk oriented, takes much time to prove themselves and need big amount of money for processing and development.

Effectiveness of VC System

As we know very well the fact that the success of any economy and the entrepreneur duly depends on the contributions of venture capital in the present context, the financing system of the same should be very effective. Data collected in this regards is analyzed and presented in a systematic manner in Table 7.21.

Table 7.21: Effectiveness of VC System

Opinion	*Respondents*	%
Satisfactory	3	60
Not Satisfactory	2	40
Total	5	100

Source: Primary Data

It is evident from Table 7.21 that the effectiveness of VC system in India is satisfactory according to the opinion of the respondent companies (60 %). Whereas, in the case of other respondents (40%) opinion it is not so, due to longer gestation period, high risk high return game, and critical aspects of VC Financing System in India.

Opinion on Exit Route

In Venture Capital type of financing exit route plays a dominant role. So data pertaining to the same is collected and analysed as far as the opinions of the respondents are concerned in Table 7.22.

Table 7.22: Opinion on Exit route

	Exit route	*Respondents*	%
1	Through IPO	2	66.667
2	Depending upon situation	1	33.333
	Total	3	100

Source: Primary Data

Low Penetration of Venture Capital

Though venture capital is a boon for entrepreneurs in biotechnology, it has not achieved a significant level of penetration in the Biotech industry. It is due to various reasons as clearly analyzed and shown in Table 7. 23.

Table 7.23: Why biotech firms are not fully aware of VC?

	Opinion	*Respondents*	%
1	Fear of getting funds*	3	60
2	Lack of awareness	2	40
	Total	5	100

* Other two companies are in pipeline of VC finance.
Source: Primary Data

It is evident from Table 7.23, that the low penetration of VC in Biotech sector is due to less significant awareness of biotech firms about VC, because of two particular reasons, they are: (1) Fear of getting funds as gestation period is very long, and (2) Lack of awareness. Hence, by conducting seminars and workshops, this awareness levels can be improved.

8

Towards a New Framework of Financing Biotechnology

Backdrop

Biotechnology is destined to be one of the prime determinants of our life styles and of the way we think and react to situations in the present century and the next. Like any such prime determinants such as space science, new sources of energy, new materials, computers, microelectronics, robotics, automation and artificial intelligence in history mankind can use biotechnology either wisely to maximize benefit to the largest number of people around the world.

Biotechnology is considered as a "dual-use" technology in the developed world as the regulatory issues become very important before an entrepreneur ventures into the biotech sector i.e., the understanding of regulatory framework becomes very important not only to the entrepreneur but for investors too.

Unlike other sectors, Life Sciences rely on vast product and service revenue potential with a huge end user market. Asia with large unmet medical needs, unresolved diseases endemic to the region and demographics, presents such an opportunity to the Life Sciences industry. A generally benign regulatory environment, China's accession to WTO and compliance with TRIPS and India's adoption of product patents from 2005 can be expected to spur investments and cross border collaborations. While governments in Singapore, China, and Taiwan are vying with each other to lead in the area with large investments. India is yet to see a concentrated government effort, though the development of the biotech industry remains on its agenda.

Biotechnology industry showed many signs of evolving into a mature industry. Numbers of products, revenues, profits, market cap are all up and show intrinsic value. The industry was trumpeted as the "greenshoots" of investment and stock market recovery in Europe and the US as more biotech-derived products came to the market. Half of the new drugs approved by the US FDA in 2003 were biologics. The industry ended the year 2003 building a diverse portfolio of protein therapeutics, many of which achieved blockbuster status. Though there was a decline in the total number of biotech companies both in the US and Europe, those surviving appears to have a firm financial base with a more realistic product portfolio.

Market capital of US biotech industry increased from $ 219 billion in 2002 to $ 342 billion in 2003. US capital markets invested $ 16 billion in biotech in 2003 as against $ 10 billion in 2002. Life Sciences sector attracted 27 per cent of all VC funding in 2003 in the US—the highest proportion in the last 12 years. There were over 155 drugs in the market, 19 approved in 2003 and over 370 drugs were in various stages of clinical trials are awaiting FDA approval.

Countries that have shown leadership in biotechnology have seen their governments commit substantial public funds. The US, Canada, UK, Germany, Ireland, Australia and Israel government have invested billions of dollars to support emerging biotechnology developments, often in partnership with the private sector. Closer home, Japanese, Korean, Taiwanese and Singaporean governments actively promote and provide seed capital for biotechnology start up companies. Singapore has identified biomedical services as the next driver in its economic growth plan and has invested over $ 2 billion into creating a world-class infrastructure and establishing the regulatory framework. In addition to providing direct seed funding and fiscal incentives, it is encouraging foreign scientists to join its government research programs in an attempt to create critical mass in its talent pool as also enable research collaborations.

India has already developed competence in selected areas and policy that provide the entrepreneurs an edge over other countries to sẹt up viable and competitive biotech industry in certain areas. With its large resource pool of modern/molecular biologists, statisticians and software programmers. India seems well placed to garner most of the biotech market. Many Indian companies have introduced products of original research through technology transfer from R&D institutions of India in the field of vaccines, diagnostics and reagents. Some others have teamed up with foreign technologies with a view to introduce them into the Indian market within the framework of Indian laws. This situation is satisfactory to begin with, but there is tremendous scope to come up with innovative products that would be original and that would have cutting edge impact in the global context. Fresh investments of about US $ 1 billion in India could hold the potential of providing turnover of US $ 1.5 to 2 billion during the next 5 to 7 years, that could contribute import substitution, augmentation of local production and introduction of some new products for global marketing in the areas such as diagnostics, vaccines therapeutics, pharmacogenomics, bioinformatics, agriculture biotechnology, Industrial biotechnology, Inputs to the industry (hardware suppliers—instrumentation and chemicals), marine bioprospecting and environment focused biotechnology. India is expected to emerge as a strong player in both manufacturing and consumption market of biotech products in the coming years.

While the biotech industry in India grew at 40 per cent during 2003-04, the country also witnessed the successful IPO of India's largest biotech company - Biocon which created excitement on two counts - creating a benchmark of Venture Capital (VC) success and sector valuation.

Indian biotech industry, like the regular pharma industry is pursuing the generics route. Biogenerics is still at a very nascent stage and there's huge opportunity ahead.

With the development of science, there is an increasing tilt towards biotech products, hence by getting into biogenetics much early than Indian companies actually did for the regular chemistry based molecules, provides for lots of untapped market potential also, this early start provides the capability build-up the entrepreneurs to graduate quickly into new drug discovery space in biotech.

Innovative biotech companies have focused more on hitting the market, rather than get the 'cost' and 'quality' equation right. The high development cost offers them entry barriers in less developed but relatively large volume markets and the not so great process/product quality provides enough scope for the generic player to exploit while seeking generic drug approvals. Thus biogeneric companies have the 'cost', 'quality' scope to surge ahead.

Venture capital is only the way of promoting and developing the biotechnologies for the betterment of the society as biotechnology is the cutting edge for venture capital in the present context. But before putting their hand, venture capitalists should understand well the Strength and Weakness as well as the benefits that they get from government in terms of incentives. Not only that, the venture capital funds needs good human resource having expertise knowledge and specializing in specific biotechnologies, finance, marketing and technology forecasting.

Scarcity of venture capital remained India's key challenge in developing the biotech industry. With the exception of few VC's, most VC's in the country are fairly new to this sector, do not quite understand the issues, are averse to risk and gestation periods involved, unlike in the US and Europe where a deep VC industry has developed with many biotech sector focused funds.

Venture capital funding of about Rs. 3000 million has been estimated for the biotech sector in the days to come. Small Industries Development Bank of India (SIDBI) and Indian Credit and Investment Corporation of India (ICICI) have committed about 35 per cent each. Banks still remain the major financing source for biotechnology with venture capital accounting for less than 20 per cent of funding.

Foreign VCs are wary of investing in Indian Biotechnology blaming the present patents regime which excludes product patenting. However, compliance with TRIPS from 2005 is expected to see greater VC support for Indian biotechnology.

Many biotech companies have adopted a services model much along the lines of the IT sector. Others have pursued a product based business model where vaccines and biogenerics dominate. A few companies have been set up as Indian arms of U.S. and European biotech companies. Very few have been able to raise venture capital to fund original R&D based business models and interestingly almost all these have a U.S. base through which they have raised capital from U.S. venture funds. The total project investment made by private biotech companies in India is estimated at $100 million over the last five years of which VC funding is only $15 million. This indicates that a large part of the funding has come from conventional sources like banks and financial institutions. Projected investment in this sector is expected to treble over the next three years.

Cost of setting up and sustaining a biotech facility is extremely high and turn around time for product development and financial return is long (VCs used to the slam-bang returns of the IT industry, may not have nerve for such long gestation).

There are not enough real experts around in the biotech field in India, hence, VCs may not get the right read on potential biotech projects nor track them, also long gestation and complex technology involved, can make the available 'expert talent' deceptive—big Ph.D. and long list of publications may not necessarily mean ability to create value and generate income regulatory mechanism for biogenerics, which is still in the formative stage, adding more to the risks.

There is lot of awareness about VC to the entrepreneurs of the biotechnology industry, but there is no full awareness about VC and its help in developing a biotechnology due to fear of getting funds and lack of awareness of the ways and means of getting VC.

Most of the Biotech companies got awareness about Venture Capital and specific information pertaining to the VC funds from which they have drawn money through corporate news and journals, financial analysts , advisors and consultants.

Investees' has the understanding about VC as capital investment for only high tech projects as well as unexploited innovative ideas.

Most of the Biotechnology companies (80%) approached the VCCs through financial analysts, advisors and consultants. A few of Biotech companies approached VCCs personally and realized about the objectives of VC and ways and means of getting such capital.

VCCs generally base upon certain critical factors for selection of any project for extending Venture finance. Through the study, it is found that the critical factors of project selection by VCCs are: technological capabilities and viability of the product, feasibility and past record of the company and multiplicity of the products.

Most of the Biotech companies are at early stage finance of Venture Capital. It is very critical stage where success or failure of the technology to be developed will lie down. Two companies out of the sample companies of study are at early stage and the rest of the companies are at prototype stage.

In general, entrepreneurs face lot of problems in getting Venture finance as VC is at take off stage in India. It is found through the study that the difficulties that were experienced by the respondent companies are trust in new entrepreneurs, by VCCs, problems faced by VCCs in similar investment, higher interest rates, delay in sanction, collateral security and looking for returns without any gestation period.

While extending the Venture finance to a project, VCs look for different qualities in entrepreneurs. They are; commitment, truthfulness, capitation to convert ideas into reality, feasibility and return on investment, new developmental works which can lead to patents and technology and previous background.

Investees of APIDC Venture Capital Fund and IDBI Venture Capital Fund felt that the commercialization of venture capital is average and the role play of their VCC Funds is satisfactory as the management style of those funds was found as strategic partner in nature.

It is found through the responses of the selected Venture Capital undertaking that they got venture finance from respective companies as their projects are very innovative and having great potentiality. Also, it is found that the competitors of such biotech companies are Banglore Genie Sigma Group, GSK Serum Institute, Roche, Bharat Biotech, in domestic market and Microsynt Organics, Wruchardt, LG Life Sciences and Jhonsons and Jhonsons in the overseas market.

As VC is quite different to traditional type of finance, the success of undertaking will depend not only on the entrepreneur but also the Venture Capitalist. Study reveals that the VC funds have rendered different additional services to Biotech undertakings in terms of marketing and strategic services, moral support and building the corporate image through existing clientele, arranging meetings and giving an approach to meet the government officials besides investing money.

Almost all the respondents opined that the role of their Venture Capital company is very proactive in supporting them with a need based financial assistance and leveraging their capabilities. So that the respondents would like to continue their association with the existing VCCs at least for five years.

Most of the respondents opined that the performance of their venture is good and satisfactory as they got adequate services from Venture Capitalists and the other required services for free of cost rendered by the Venture Capitalists. So, they feel the effectiveness of VC system is very satisfactory. On the whole, according to the opinion of the selected biotech companies financed by VCCs as respondents, the role play of venture capital in their ventures is satisfactory. It is due to such level of satisfaction they ranked the VCCs as good in role play as Venture Capital Companies.

The opinion of respondents revealed that the Venture Capital is a boon for technocrats' particularly first generation entrepreneurs and the economy for achieving high level of growth.

In Biotechnology financing, APIDC Venture Capital Ltd. is ahead of other Venture Capital Funds viz., ICICI, IDBI, SIDBI and others in Andhra Pradesh.

As the critical aspect of Venture Capital is exit strategy, most of the respondent companies (67%) are preferring to use the IPO as the best route for exit of their VCCs from the ventures.

The penetration of venture capital in Biotech industry is not so high due to lack of awareness and fear of getting funds from VCCs as gestation period is so high. But in the days to come Venture Capital will be the only solution for Development and Promotion of Biotechnology.

There is much knowledge gap to Venture Capitalist as far as biotechnology is concerned. Because biotechnology is part of science and dynamic in nature, so VCs cannot understand immediately the implications of technology that is to be developed and how much time will it take to develop itself, even for that matter the entrepreneurs also. Not only that even VCs are not making a forward step in BT ventures like others as they are not so confident about the immediate results of such technologies. Hence, VCs need to get inputs from scientists and professors of BT from various Research Institutions and Universities rather than depending upon only their project managers.

Financing Biotechnology: A New Framework

If India is determined not to miss the next big industrial wave, biotechnology, it is imperative to evolve strong fiscal and regulatory policies that support entrepreneurship, low cost base for research and manufacturing and encourage investments into the sector.

A national biotech and bioinformatics policy by January 2005, compliance with the global regime on intellectual property rights, quadrilateral agreement between the academia, industry, laboratories and the state and addressing the procedural issues which the government has already initiated through some positive measures, but still there are some measures are in due with Government as concessions and exemptions given to IT sector. Further the policy should also address specific issues in relation to biotechnology and also outline the future strategy and road map. They are: Promotion of research and development, technology transfer and commercialization, public-private partnership, capacity building, human resources development, infrastructure strengthening, international cooperation regulatory framework, biosafety, IPR, trade and investment, social and ethical issues and communication and public awareness.

Biotechnology is a part and parcel of India's science and technology policy. What is needed is to implement the first vision document (2003 Science and Technology Policy) for five years. This would help to create a knowledge based society, thrust on institutional development, poverty alleviation, large projects of societal upliftment, intensify research, convert leads to products, processes and technology and benefit the poorest of the poor.

As the biotech industry is a promising one and helps the economy a lot, the central and the state governments could even consider buying equity in some of the biotechnology industries in the country that could be done through the state aided financial institutions.

In the BT sector, there is a need for influx of venture capitalists (VCs) in a big way. The government has to open up the sector and attract a lot of foreign direct investment (FDI).

VCs need to stride carefully on the biotech space as of now; they need to have a closer view of the project, rather than take a angel position.

They need to also have real experts from the advanced countries to do Due Diligence before investment and a technical expert oversee product development IT type start-up approach to biotech may not necessarily be a successful and the present players are fragmented in their expertise. So, VCs can explore bringing together such fragmented players and leverage their venture activities. On the other hand, one opportunity on which the VCs can bet their money on Custom Biological Services, that is those business models which will provide development services to the biotech players of the advanced countries which helps to build own capabilities in the long run, while providing scope for shorter turnaround time for revenues.

As Venture Capital penetration is very low in India due to traditional financier role play of some of the venture capital funds and longer gestation period as a chronic problem of biotech industry and others, there is a need to move from Earth to Heaven both the Government as well as the Venture Capital Funds in developing policy and framework very suitable for the biotechnology industry, as it is going to rule the economy in the days to come, like other technologies.

VCCs should play very proactive role in promoting the new and budding entrepreneurs having sound knowledge in biotechnology, because, Venture Capital is only solution for exploiting new and innovative ideas that comes from such type of entrepreneurs.

VCCs need to conduct some seminars and workshops at different places of country to make the potential entrepreneurs/ technocrats of biotech sector aware about Venture Capital and its role in Development and Promotion of biotechnology through Venture Capital.

Schematic Approach

We discuss below the systems design approach for creating a new framework for biotechnology financing which encompasses its various elements and presents a radically different way of solving complex Problems of biotechnology in a business like way.

Summing up

Biotechnology holds the key to the growth of mankind and nations in future. Although, it is a high growth business, it is equally risky and full of volatility. VC financing assures the growth element in biotechnology and takes away its risk element which makes it business friendly. If India has to benefit from Biotechnology to the fullest scale, it has to design and implement such public policies which create abundance of VC financing and make it a hub of such institutions.

Schematic Approach for Financing Biotechnology

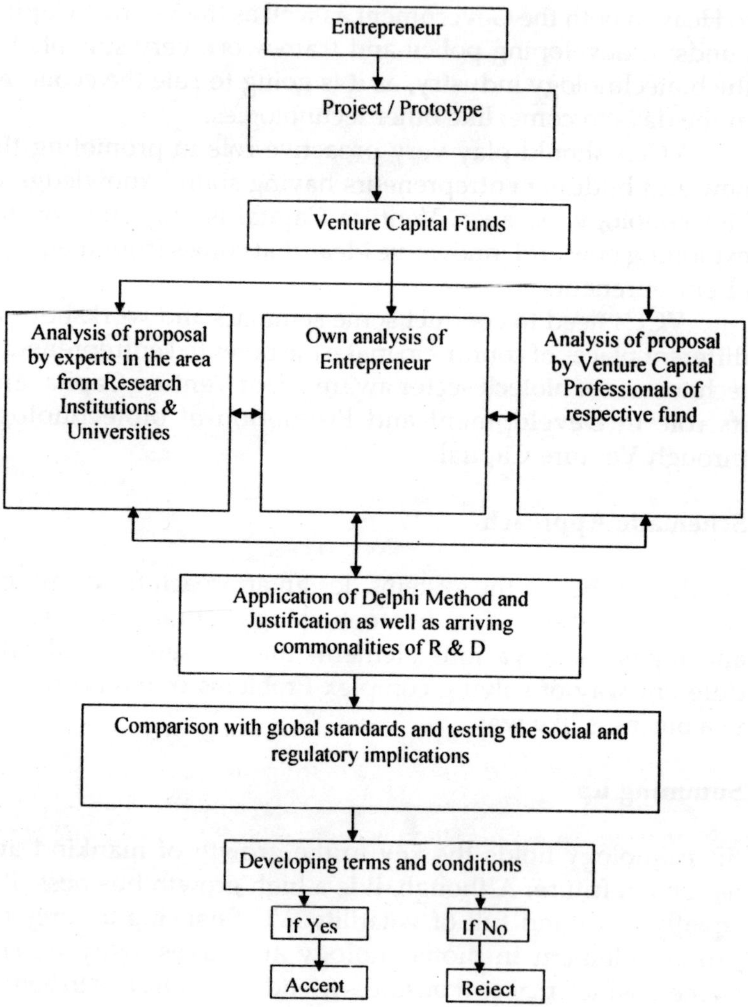

9

A Case Study of M/s Jayaprada Clonetech Private Limited

Introduction

M/s Jayaprada Clonetech (P) Ltd., a new company promoted by Dr. A. Jayaprada and associates propose to set up a unit for manufacturing biotechnology pharmaceutical products i.e., Monoclonal antibody (Mab) based Diagnostic Kits for Thyroid and pituitary hormones and insulin at Uppal Village, Ranga Reddy district, Andhra Pradesh with an installed capacity of 8000 kits per annum. The technology for the project is developed by Dr. Jayaprada. The project was originally appraised by Industrial Development Bank of India-Technology Fund (IDBI-TF) under its Venture Capital Fund (VCF) scheme in September, 1990. The project cost was estimated as Rs. 77.00 lakhs and IDBI sanctioned a VCF term loan of Rs. 65.00 lakhs and APIDC sanctioned an equity assistance of Rs.1.80 lakhs. During the implementation IDBI felt that though the project progress is satisfactory and is expected to be completed earlier than the originally envisaged time frame, there is expected to be some overrun in the cost of the project. Subsequently in December 1991 IDBI-TF re-appraised the project and re-estimated the project cost as Rs. 147.00 lakhs resulting in a cost overrun of Rs. 70 lakhs. IDBI sanctioned an additional VCF term loan of Rs. 37.90 lakhs totaling its assistance to Rs. 102.90 lakhs. IDBI increased the promoter's contribution from Rs. 12.00 lakhs in the original proposal (15.6% of the project cost) to Rs. 44.10 lakhs in the revised proposal (30% of the project cost). APIDC recently sanctioned an additional equity assistance of Rs. 4.80 lakhs to the company. The Promoters are well qualified and first generation entrepreneurs with limited means and therefore approached APIDC-VCL to bridge the gap in equity in view of the sharp increase in project cost for reasons beyond their control. The project cost of Rs. 147.00 lakhs including a working capital margin of Rs. 10.00 lakhs, is proposed to be financed by equity share capital of Rs. 44.10 lakhs, and Rs. 102.90 lakhs of VCF term loan from IDBI. Out of the equity of Rs. 44.10 lakhs private promoters are expected to bring in Rs. 30.20 lakhs and APIDC sanctioned Rs. 6.60 lakhs leaving a gap of Rs. 7.30 lakhs. Therefore, the company sought an assistance of Rs. 7.50 lakhs from APIDC-VCL towards direct subscription to the equity of the company.

Background of the Company/Promoters Company:

M/s Jayaprada (P) Ltd. was incorporated as Private Limited company under Companies Act, 1956 in September 1990 with its registered office in Hyderabad. The authorised share capital of the company is Rs.10.00 lakhs.

Promoters: The promoter directors of the company are:

		Age (Yrs.)
1.	Dr. A. Jayaprada	62
2.	Dr. B. Srikanth	30
3.	Shri C. Nageswar Rao	28
4.	Smt. D. Sri Devi	24

- Dr. A. Jayaprada: Ph.D. in Genetics (She is an eminent Bio-Technologist. She has widely travelled. She has published many research papers and guided 50 PH.D. Students.)
- Dr. B.Srikanth: MBBS . (He is a general practitioner holding a Diploma in Orthopedics and has worked on monoclonal antibodies. He is nephew of Dr.A. Jayaprada.
- Sri. C. Nageswar Rao: Final Year Student of MBBS (He is the son-in-law of Dr. A. Jayaprada).
- Smt. D. Sri Devi: Studying B.Tech. (Electronics)(She is the daughter of Dr.A. Jayaprada.)

Management Capability

Dr. A. Jayaprada will be the Managing Director of the company. The company has rallied a good team of qualified technical personnel to carry out the developmental work. Under the direct supervision of Dr. Jayaprada, the following personnel are carrying out the development work.

(i) Prof. A.V. Reddy — M.Sc., Ph.D., (Animal Genetics)
(ii) Mrs. A . Nirmala — M.Sc. (Bio Chemistry)
(iii) Mrs. B. Vimala — M.Sc. (Zoology)
(iv) Miss. I. Kamala — M.Sc. (Bio Chemistry)
(v) Shri Ram Manohar — M.Sc. (Genetics)
(vi) Shri S. K. Rao — M.Sc. (Bio Chemistry)

The company has already succeeded in developing the following MAbs, using certain facilities available with research institutions such as University of Hyderabad and JNTU:

Item	*Quantity (mgs)*	*ELISA Plates (nos.) (32 wells)*
T3	15	4500
T4	20	6000
Tsh	20	6000
Insulin	10	3000

Dr. Jayaprada, also indicated that the research team has achieved a near breakthrough in developing diagnostic kits for ascertaining pregnancy at a very early stage.

Shareholding Pattern

Out of the proposed total equity of Rs.44.10 lakhs, the promoters would mobilise Rs.30.00 lakhs, (68% of the equity). The proposed shareholding pattern is as follows:

Equity	*Rs. in lakhs*	*Percentage*
Dr A Jayaprada	6.00	13.60
Dr B Srikanth	1.80	4.08
Sri C Nageshwar Rao	2.40	5.44
Smt D Sri Devi	1.80	4.08
Friends and Associates	18.19	41.30
	30.20	**68.50**
APIDC	6.60	15.00
APODC-VCL (proposed)	7.30	16.50
	44.10	100.00

Project Proposal

The company proposes to manufacture diagnostic kits for T3, T4, TSH, LH, Prolactin and Insulin hormones with an installed capacity of 8000 kits per annum. T3 and T4 hormones are secreted by thyroid gland and their secretion, is controlled by thyroid stimulating hormone (TSH) secreted by pituitary gland. Any change in their concentration in body results in disorders related to overall metabolism of body and heart, since these hormones control theses activities. Follicle stimulating hormone (FSH), Leutenising hormone (LH) and prolactin are secreted by pituitary gland and control various functions of reproductive system of the body. Insulin is secreted by specific cells of pancreas gland and controls sugar levels in blood. Hence, measurement of these hormone levels in body would help both in diagnosis as well as monitoring the treatment of disorders related to these hormones. RIA method involves radioisotopes and needs special facilities as well as greater care in handling and disposing EIA, using monoclonal antibodies, is more specific and sensitive than ETA with polyclonal antibodies.

The company has developed EIA kit based on monoclonal antibodies for FSH, got it tested by some diagnostic centres in Hyderabad and has found it satisfactory. Technology for other hormone kits (which is akin to FSH) i.e. T3, T4, TSH, LH, Prolactin and Insulin is also developed.

Dr. A, who has vast experience in the area of Genetics has developed the technology for the diagnostic kits based on monoclonal antibody systems. The trial kits developed by

Dr. Jayaprada are tested at the Medvin Endocrine Diagnostic Centre in Hyderabad. The Diagnostic Centre informed that the trial kits are quite comparable with the imported STG Immuno Assay Kits.

Project Cost

Estimated cost of the project is Rs.147.00 lakhs. The details are given below:

(Rs. in lakh)

	IDBI's Revised Estimate	*Expenditure incurred*
Land and Site Development	4.56	4.56
Building and Civil Works	27.54	31.89
Plant and Machinery (imported)		
Plant and Machinery (indigenous)	17.48	36.35
Erection and Commissioning	0.20	
Miscellaneous Fixed Assets	14.65	9.33
Operating Expenses	14.00	17.48
Prelim and Pre OP expenses	7.00	8.37
Marketing Exp.	4.00	0.18
Contingencies	2.00	-
Interest during Development Period	8.24	3.12
Margin money for WC	10.00	-*
Total	146.86	116.52

* Cash and bank balance and bank guarantees provided include Rs.5.24 lakhs.

Means of Finance

(Rs. in lakhs)

	Revised Proposal	*Money Raised*
Equity		
PROMOTERS	30.20	28.39
APIDC	6.60	4.80
APIDC-VCL (Proposed)	7.30	—
	44.10	33.19
Loans		
IDBI—VCF Term Loan	102.90	83.00
Total	147.00	116.19*

* Rs. 0.33 lakhs are earned as interest on STDs, which is not included above.

Reasons for Overrun

There is an overrun of Rs.70 lakhs in the project cost (91% of the original project cost). The major reasons for overrun as given by IDBI are as follows:

(i) **Land(+ Rs.2.06 lakhs):** The company could not succeed in procuring 2 acres of land as one plot and it was forced to go in for 3.15 acres of land in an industrial area in Ranga Reddy District, at a cost of Rs.1.3 lakhs per acre.

(ii) **Civil Construction (+ Rs.14.24 lakhs):** It was originally envisaged that the factory would have a covered area of 5400 sq.ft. @ Rs. 246/sq.ft. Due to general increase in cost of building materials, the cost of civil construction has gone up to Rs.278 sq.ft. (by about Rs.2 lakhs). Moreover, the company decided to construct additional area of 4510 sq.ft. (@ Rs.278 sq.ft.) as the earlier provision made for laboratory and animal house was highly inadequate.

(iii) **Plant and Machinery (+ Rs.26.47 lakhs):** The variation in the cost of major items of plant and machinery could be broadly categorised as follows:

(Rs. in lakhs)

Particulars	*Original*	*Revised*	*Increase*
Imported equipment escalation due to devaluation of rupee	16.90	26.88	(+) 9.98
Equipment purchased on rupee payment instead of importing them as originally envisaged	5.70	5.00	(-) 0.70
Escalation due to General price and Customs duty	5.60	9.10	(+) 3.50
Additional equipment now required			
—Imported	—	5.31	(+) 5.31
—Indigenous	—	8.38	(+) 8.38
	28.20	54.67	26.47

(iv) **Misc. Fixed Assets (+ Rs. 9.65 lakhs):** Details of original and revised estimates are as follows:

(Rs. in lakhs)

	Original	*Revised*
Generator set (50 KVA) (originally envisaged 6 KVA)	0.40	2.44
Air Conditioners (for mice room, manufacturing area, biochemistry and immunology)	0.50	4.17
Clean room facilities	—	2.70
Cold storage room	—	0.94
Furniture	0.40	1.00
Vehicle	3.70	1.99
Computer	—	1.41
	5.0	14.65

(v) **Operating expenses (+ Rs.6.4 lakhs) and Preliminary and Pre-operative expenses (+ Rs.4.10 lakhs):** Based on the expenses incurred upto end-October, 1991, reasonable estimates have been made to cover the expenditure likely to be incurred upto December, 1992—the tentative period for completion of the venture.

Market

IDBI has estimated the demand for T3, T4, TSH, LH, Prolactin and Insulin hormones kits is about 5000 kits each per year. All the immuno diagnostic kits are being imported as there is no indigenous producers. The traditional methods for diagnostic of diseases have certain disadvantages like low specificity requirement and costly and sophisticated equipment, etc. on the other monoclonal antibody diagnostic kits developed by the company have the advantageous of high specificity, long shelf life, high sensitivity, simplicity in operation, reproduceable result and cost effectiveness. The cost of the imported kits is around Rs.6000 per kit as against the selling price of 4500 per kit of the company. The substantial difference in the cost of the kit in addition to the hefty margins offered to the dealers and may push the product in the market without much difficulty.

Important Financial Indicators

Parameters	*1994*	*1995*	*1996*	*1997*
Installed Capacity (Kits/Annum)	8000.00	8000.00	8000.00	8000.00
Capacity Utilisation (%)	50.00	60.00	75.00	75.00
Production (Kits/Annum)	4000.00	4800.00	6000.00	6000.00
Total Income (Rs. lakhs)	180.00	216.00	270.00	270.00
Raw Materials/ Income (%)	25.00	25.00	25.00	25.00
Interest/Income(%)	15.89	11.48	8.74	7.70
Net Profit/Income (%)	–2.06	3.84	7.04	6.74
Operating BEP (%)		53.00		
Project IRR (%)		33.00		
EPS (RS)	–0.84	1.88	4.31	4.13
Return on APIDC-VCL Equity (%)		18.80		

Expected Returns to APIDC-VCL

The proposed financial assistance is Rs.7.30 lakhs as direct subscription to equity of the company. The expected returns on equity are as follows:

(Rs. in lakhs)

Year of Operation	*Year*	% Dividend	*Amount*	*Book* Value (Rs.)	*Disinvest-ment*	*Total*
I	1993-94	0	0	9.16	—	—
II	1994-95	0	0	11.04	—	—
III	1995-96	0	0	15.35	—	—
IV	1996-97	19	1.387	17.57	—	1.387
V	1997-98	19	1.387	19.57	—	1.387
VI	1998-99	19	1.387	21.27	—	1.387
VII	1999-2000	19	0	22.63	16.52	16.520
			4.161		16.52	20.681

Disinvestment is assumed in the 7th year by APIDC-VCL. Buy back/disinvestment prices are calculated based on Book value in the year of disinvestment. The expected returns to APIDC-VCL in such a case is 18.80 per cent. The actual disinvestment by APIDC-VCL would be made based on a fair price calculated at the time of disinvestment and the first option of buying back the shares would be given to the Promoters. It can be seen that the expected returns to APIDC-VCL is quite low. This is mainly because the company has to service VCF term loan of Rs.102.90 lakhs by way of interest @ 18.5 per cent after the commercial production and royalty on sales at 5 per cent giving them an over all return of around 33 per cent.

Schedule of Implementation

Civil construction is completed in March 1992 and the majority of the machinery are received and installed. The company has completed the developmental work of the kits in December 1991 and the kits are trial tested till April 1992 and the commercial release of the kits into the market is expected by the end of June 1992.

Conclusions and Recommendations

M/s A. Jayaprada Clontech (P) Ltd., a new company promoted by Dr. A. Jayaprada and Associates, proposes to set up a unit for manufacturing biotechnology pharmaceutical products i.e. Monoclonal Antibody (MAb) based Diagnostic kits for Thyroid and pituitary hormones and insulin at Uppal Village, Ranga Reddy District, Andhra Pradesh with an installed capacity of 8000 kits per annum. The technology for the project is developed by Dr. A. Jayaprada. The project is originally appraised by IDBI Technology Fund (TF) under its Venture Capital Fund scheme in September 1990. The project cost was estimated as Rs. 77.00 lakhs and IDBI sanctioned an VCF term loan of Rs. 65.00 lakhs and APIDC sanctioned an equity assistance of Rs. 1.80 lakhs. During the implementation IDBI felt that though the project progress is satisfactory and is expected to be completed earlier than the originally envisaged time frame, there is expected to be some overrun in the cost of the project. Subsequently in December 1991 IDBI-TF re-appraised the project cost as Rs.147.00 lakhs resulting in a cost overrun of Rs. 70 lakhs. IDBI sanctioned an additional VCF term loan of Rs. 37.90 lakhs totaling its assistance to Rs. 102.90 lakhs.

IDBI increased the promoters contribution from Rs.12.00 lakhs in the original proposal (15.6% of the project cost) to 44.1 lakhs in the revised proposal (30% of the project cost). APIDC recently sanctioned an additional equity assistance of Rs.4.80 lakhs to the company. The promoters are technically well qualified, experienced and are first generation entrepreneurs with limited means. The project involves indigenous development of diagnostic kits based on monoclonal antibody systems. The demand for the product is quite good and the indigenous requirement is being met by imports. The project is ready for commercialisation. The expected returns to APIDC-VCL are around 18.80 per cent which are quite low. In view of the foregoing, the company's request for Venture Capital assistance of Rs. 7.30 lakhs in the form of direct subscription to equity of the company subject to the standard terms and conditions given in Annexure-I is placed before the Investment Committee for guidance and sanction.

Issues for Discussion

In the light of the facts mentioned and information provided, the following issues merit further discussion: (1) Do M/s Jayaprada Clonetech (P) Ltd. qualify for inclusion in the Venture Capital portfolio? Comment on the nature of Terms of Reference laid down by APIDC for extending equity support to APIDC-VCL (2) To what extent is the company's management structure professional? Is family owned management structure ideal to organise a Venture Capital company? (3) Is the existing pattern of project appraisal by APIDC-VCL and IDBI appropriate? Should there be multiple evaluations of the same project by the Venture Capital Funds? (4) Is the process of project appraisal suitable to examine the Venture Capital proposals? (5) Is the rate of return estimated for M/s Jayaprada Clonetech (P) Ltd. adequate for it to be accepted by APIDC-VCL and IDBI? (6) Are time and cost overruns in the case of M/s Jayaprada Clonetech (P) Ltd. justified in the existing frame of situation? (7) Is there a need to privatise M/s Jayaprada Clonetech (P) Ltd ? If yes, then work out the modalities for privatisation.

ANNEXURE-I

Terms and Conditions for Equity Participation

1. The company shall carry out such alterations to its Memorandum and the Articles of Association in consultation with and to the satisfaction of APIDC-VCL so as to safeguard the interests of APIDC-VCL arising out of its assistance granted to the company.
2. The company/promoters shall enter into a suitable investment agreement with APIDC-VCL to the satisfaction of APIDC-VCL.
3. The company shall produce permission/clearance from the appropriate government agency for setting up the unit.
4. The company shall raise its authorised capital upto Rs. 50.00 lakhs.
5. The subscribed share capital of the company shall be Rs. 44.10 lakhs.
6. The contribution of the private promoters shall not be less than Rs. 30.20 lakhs in the equity share capital of the company. The contribution by the APIDC-VCL shall be made on pro-rata basis with that of the contribution of the promoters and their associates in the equity share capital of the company after obtaining necessary clearances from financial institutions and other government agencies. APIDC-VCL shall release its share of contribution only after the shares subscribed and paid up to the extent of 100 per cent of its promoters' contribution towards equity of the company.

7a. The promoter directors shall give an undertaking to the APIDC-VCL in such form as may be prescribed by the APIDC-VCL that they shall procure for the company such additional finances as may be required to meet the shortfall, if any, in financing the project and/or for working capital. The funds brought in shall not be withdrawn without the prior approval of APIDC-VCL.

7b. The company/promoter directors shall make necessary arrangements to the satisfaction of APIDC-VCL for raising a term loan to the extent of Rs.102.90 lakhs required for financing the project from Banks/other financial institutions.

8. The company/promoter directors shall not raise any further term loans/deposits other than the amount of Rs. 102. 90 lakhs as mentioned above except with the specific written approval of the APIDC-VCL.

9. It shall be the responsibility of the company to raise short term borrowings from scheduled bank for working capital requirements of the company.

10. The actual expenditure incurred by the promoters for the project shall be subject to the scrutiny and approval of the APIDC-VCL.

11. The company shall not without the proper consent and written approval of the APIDC-VCL pay any commission to its promoter directors or concerns in which directors are interested and for furnishing guarantees for any financial assistance obtained by the company for the purpose of its project.

12. The company shall broadbase the Board and finalise the composition of its Board of Directors to the satisfaction of the APIDC-VCL.

13. (a) APIDC-VCL shall have the right to appoint and remove from time to time, director (s), on the Board of Directors of the company; such director(s) is (are) hereinafter referred to as 'Nominee Director (s)', so long as the APIDC-VCL holds shares in the equity, as a result of direct subscription.

(b) The number of directors to represent APIDC-VCL on the company Board shall be in promotion to the APIDC-VCL's shareholding in the company with a minimum of one director and the APIDC-VCL's nominees shall not be required to hold any qualification shares.

(c) At least one of the nominees of the APIDC-VCL shall be non-rotational director. The articles of association of the company shall contain suitable provisions in this behalf.

If, at any time, the Nominee Director is not able to attend a meeting of the Board of Directors or any of its Committees, of which he is a member, APIDC-VCL may depute an Observer to attend the meeting. The expenses incurred by APIDC-VCL in this connection shall be borne by the company.

14. Provided however, APIDC-VCL shall have the liberty and discretion to appoint such directors immediately after the acceptance of the letter of intent by the company, but such appointment shall not be construed as any commitment on the part of the APIDC-VCL to disburse the financial assistance unless the APIDC-VCL is fully satisfied that the company has compiled with all the stipulated terms and conditions precedent to such disbursement.
15. The Managing Director of the company shall be the nominee of the promoter of the company who shall be appointed to the satisfaction of the APIDC-VCL.
16. The APIDC-VCL reserves to itself the right to inspect the factory, properties and assets, documents and records, books and accounts etc. of the company during the period the APIDC-VCL holds shares in the company.
17. The company shall keep the APIDC-VCL informed in such manner and in such form as may be prescribed by the APIDC-VCL from time to time of the progress made in the implementation of the project and of the working of the same and also of any expenditure/ diversification thereof, as long as the APIDC-VCL holds any shares in the company. The company shall furnish to the APIDC-VCL all additional information, data, documents and explanations as may be called by the APIDC-VCL in relation to the working and affairs.

18. The company shall furnish to the APIDC-VCL all notices in respect of the Board Meetings, shareholders meetings of the company together with notes and minutes thereof in addition to the circulation of the same to the nominees of the APIDC-VCL on the Board of the company.
19. The Management of the company shall vest in the Board of Directors and the day-to-day affairs shall be entrusted to the Managing Director/Committee of Directors.
20. The Promoter directors shall not transfer, dispose off or pledge or in any way encumber their shareholdings in the company without the prior consent and written approval of the APIDC-VCL and the company shall not recognise or register any such transfer of shares without the consent of the APIDC-VCL.
21. The Company shall issue the share certificates to the APIDC-VCL in marketable lots for the subscription made by it towards the equity share capital of the Company.
22. All the matters relating to the affairs of the company and the project such as capital expenditure, raising loans, awarding contracts, placement of orders for goods and services etc shall be decided by the company in consultation with the representatives of the APIDC-VCL on the Board of Directors of the company or a Committee of Directors consisting of the APIDC-VCL's nominee (s) and the Managing Director of the company and any other directors of the company.
23. Any change in the management of the company and its project shall only be made with the prior consent and written approval of the APIDC-VCL so long as the APIDC-VCL holds any shares.
24. The company shall not embark upon or undertake any new project of expansion/diversification programme without the prior approval in writing of the APIDC-VCL, so long as the APIDC-VCL holds any shares.

25. So long as the APIDC-VCL holds equity shares in the company, the company shall not, without the prior written approval of the APIDC-VCL:
    (a) Make any inter-corporate investments and/or advance/deposit monies in any other corporate bodies; and
    (b) Repay the deposits/loans that may be obtained from directors, their relatives and friends etc. for the project.
26. The company shall arrange in consultation with and to the satisfaction of the APIDC-VCL for appointment of suitable technical and managerial personnel and for provision of the necessary training facilities to them and that in matters of recruitment of personnel required to man the project, the company shall give preference to local personnel.
27. APIDC-VCL reserves to itself the right to alter, modify or change all or any of the above terms and conditions and in addition, the APIDC-VCL may impose at its discretion such further conditions as it may deem fit, for the grant/disbursal of.

ANNEXURE-II

M/s Jayaprada Clonetech Private Ltd. Cost of Production and Profitability Statement (Year Ending June 30)

(Rs. in lakhs)

	1994	*1995*	*1996*	*1997*	*1998*	*1999*	*2000*
Installed Capacity (No. of Kits/Yr.)	8000	8000	8000	8000	8000	8000	8000
Capacity Utilisation (%)	40	50	60	70	70	70	70
Production (Kits)	3200	4000	4800	5600	5600	5600	5600
Sales (value)	64.0	80.0	96.0	112.0	112.0	112.0	112.0
Cost of Production							
Raw Material	8.0	10.0	12.0	14.0	14.0	14.0	14.0
Utilities	1.0	1.2	1.4	1.7	1.7	1.7	1.7
Salaries	9.2	10.1	11.1	12.2	13.5	14.8	16.3
Repairs and Maintenance	0.9	1.0	1.1	1.2	1.3	1.4	1.6
Admn. Expenses	1.0	1.1	1.2	1.3	1.4	1.5	1.6
Selling Expenses	19.2	24.0	28.8	33.6	33.6	33.6	33.6
TOTAL	**39.3**	**47.4**	**55.6**	**64.0**	**66.5**	**67.0**	**68.8**
Profit/Loss	24.7	32.6	40.4	48.0	46.5	45.0	43.2
Interest-VCF-Bank	9.8	9.0	7..5	6.0	4.5	3.0	1.5
Depreciation	7.0	7.0	7.0	7.0	7.0	7.0	7.0
Royalty	3.2	4.0	4.8	5.6	5.6	5.6	5.6
Profit Before Tax	1.3	8.9	16.9	25.2	25.2	25.2	25.2
Tax	0.0	3.6	6.8	10.1	10.1	10.1	10.1
Net Profit	1.3	5.3	10.1	15.1	15.1	15.1	14.9
Dividend (@ 18%)	-	-	2.2	2.2	2.2	2.2	2.2
Cash accruals	8.3	12.3	14.9	19.9	19.9	19.9	19.7

Bibliography

1. Books and Research Articles

Alam Gayur (1994). 'Biotechnology and Sustainable Agriculture: Lessons from India', *OECDTechnical Paper No. 103*, Paris, France.

A.Maria, J. Ruet, M-H. Zerah, "Biotechnology in India ", Report Commissioned by the French Embassy in India.

BCIL (2001). Directory of Biotechnology Industries and Institutions in India, Biotech Consortium India Limited, New Delhi.

Bhargava, P M (1995). 'Biotechnology's Decade of Stagnation', *Economic and Political Weekly*, December 2.

Biotechnology Policy 2001, Department of Industries and Commerce, Government of Andhra Pradesh, India, April, 2001.

BINAS (2001). 'GMO Field Trials; Database of Field Trials by Country', *The Biosafety*.

Biofertiliser Statistics (2001). The Fertiliser Association of India, New Delhi.

Bownder B, 'Growth of Biotechnology Industry in India—An Evolutionary Perspective', Paper Presented at Singapore Management University, Singapore, 2003.

Brenner, Carliene and John, Komen (1994). 'International Initiatives in Biotechnology for Developing Country Agriculture: Promises and Problems', *OECD Technical Paper No. 100*.

Chaturvedi, Sachin (1997). 'Biosafety Policy and Implications in India', *Biotechnology and Development Monitor*, No. 30, March.

Chaturvedi, Sachin (1999). 'Amending Patents Act: Options Before India', *Mainstream*, March 6th.

Chaturvedi, Sachin (1999). 'The Asian Biotechnology Market: Emerging Investment Trends, AgBiotech Net, CAB International, Vol. 1, March.

Chaturvedi, Sachin (2001). 'Continued Ambiguity on GMOs', *Economic and Political Weekly*, October 20, 2001.

Chaturvedi, Sachin (2002). *'WTO, Biosafety Regulatory Regime and Trade in Genetically Modified Goods: Options before Developing Countries.*

Chaturvedi S, "*Status and Development of Biotechnology in India: An Analytical Overview*, RIS Discussion Papers, 2002

Chaturvedi, Sachin (2002). 'The Public-Private Debate in Agricultural Biotechnology and New Trends in the IPR Regime: Challenges before Developing Countries', *The Economic and Political Weekly*, March 30th.

Department of Biotechnology (1994). 'Biotechnology: Research Development and Demonstration: Thrust Areas', *Department of Biotechnology Annual Report 1993-94*, Ministry of Science and Technology, Government of India.

Department of Biotechnology (2001). *Annual Report* 2000-01, Ministry of Science and Technology, Government of India, New Delhi.

Dhar, B. and Sachin Chaturvedi (1998). 'India's Biotechnology Plans for the Next Five Years', *Biotechnology and Development Monitor*, No. 35.

Dhar, B. and Sachin Chaturvedi (1999). 'TRIPs and CBD: The Widening Gulf', *Biotechnology and Development Review, Vol 3 No. 1.*

Dosi, Giovanni, Pavitt Keith and Soete Luc (1990). 'The Economics of Technical Change and International Trade' *New York University Press.*

Ghosh, P K (1997). 'Genetically Engineered Plants in Indian Agriculture', *Journal of National Botanical Society*, Vol. 51 pp. 11-32.

Hettel, G. (1997). 'Partners Make Hybrid Rice a Reality in India', *Mimeo*, International Rice Research Institute, Manila.

Information Network and Advisory Service (BINAS), United Nations Industrial Development Organisation, retrieved from the internet: http://binas.unido.org/binas/fieldtrials.php3.

Kumar, Nagesh (1988). "Biotechnology in India", *Development* (Special issue on Biotechnology), March.

Kumar Nagesh (1998). 'India, Paris Convention and TRIPs', *Economic and Political Weekly*, September 5.

Lall, Sanjay (1992). 'Technological Capabilities and Industrialisation', *World Development*, 20: 165-186.

Mani, Sunil (1990). 'Biotechnology Research in India: Implications for Indian Public Sector Enterprises', *Economic and Political Weekly*, August 25.

McGaw, Eric M (2001). 'A Temple of Rice: Success in Biotechnology Through Networking', The Rockefeller Foundation, Hyderabad.

Mehra, K.L., (2000). 'Plant Varieties Bill Does Safeguard Farmers' Rights', *The Economic Times*, December 16.

Nelson Richard R. (ed.) (1993). 'National Innovation System: A Comparative Analysis', *Oxford University Press*, New York.

Panchamukhi, V. R. and Nagesh Kumar (1998). 'Impact on Commodity Exports' in *Biotechnology Revolution and the Third World: Challenges and Policy Options*, pp. 207-224.

Pental, Deepak (1998). 'Plant Molecular Biology and Biotechnology in India', *Plant Molecular Biology Reporter*, Vol. 16, pp. 93-97.

Perspective'. A Paper Presented in an *International Conference on Biotechnology and Development: Challenges and Opportunities for the Asian Region*, RIS, New Delhi.

Prakash, Jitendra (1997). 'The Concept of Biovillage in Proceedings of Regional Training-cum-Workshop on Application of Biotechnologies to Rainfed Farming System, including Bioindexing, emphasizing participatory approach at community level', M.S. Swaminathan Research Foundation, Chennai.

Ramanaiah, T. V. (2002). 'Indian Acts, Rules, Regulations and Procedures for handling Genetically Modified Organisms and r-DNA Products'. A Paper Presented in an *International Conference on Biotechnology and Development: Challenges and Opportunities for the Asian Region*, RIS, New Delhi.

Rao, S. R. (1999). 'Future of Biofertilisers Research, Commercialişation and Popularisation', *Department of Biotechnology*, New Delhi.

RIS data base on (i) Financial Express, 10th October 2001, (ii) Business Standard, December 24th 2000, (iii) Business line, July 9th 2001, (iv) Economist, September 1st 2001.

RIS data base on budgetary papers of relevant years, Ministry of Finance, Government of India.

Sadananda, A. R. (2002). 'Agricultural Biotechnology—An Industry Perspective'. A Paper Presented in an *International Conference on Biotechnology and Development: Challenges and Opportunities for the Asian Region*, RIS, New Delhi.

Sah, D.C. and C.G. Ranade (1983). 'Biofertilisers in Indian Agriculture—A Case Study of Gujarat', *The Economic and Political Weekly*, March 30.

Satyanarayana Chary. T: *Venture* Capital in India—An Overview, *Management Researcher*, 2000, Tiruvananthapuram.

Satyanarayana Chary. T: Venture Capital Industry—Issues and Measures for Development, *Pratibimba*, 2001.

Satyanarayana Chary. T: Venture Capital Industry, *JIMS 8M*, Nov-Dec 2001.

Satyanarayana Chary.T: Venture Capital Industry in India—An Overview, published in *Prabandh*, August 2003, Jaipur.

Satyanarayana Chary: VC Funding—Nothing ventured, nothing gained, *Business Line*, Tuesday March 30, 2004.

Satyanarayana Chary: Mission of Venture Capital in Promotion of New Enterprises—A Study, *Udyoga Prgati*, Jan-March 2005, the journal of Practicing Management, NITIE, Mumbai.

Satyanarayana Chary: Venture Capial—Concepts and Application, *Macmillan India Ltd.*, 2005.

Sethi, Sudhir (2001). 'Venture Capital Reforms: Give Me More on the Platter', *The Economic Times*, 31st January.

Sharma, Devinder (2001). 'Crisis Research: Managing Lethal Yellowing Disease', *Biotechnology and Development Monitor* No. 44/45, March 2001.

Steve Usdin, Senior Editor, "Doing Business in India", *BioCentury*, Vol 12, No.34, 2 Aug, 2004.

Visalakshi S. and G. D. Sandhya (2000). 'R&D in Pharma Industry in Context of Biotech Commercialisation', *The Economic and Political Weekly*, November 25.

Wahab, Seema (1998). 'Biotechnology and Economic of IPM in India' in *Biotechnology and Development Review* (BDR), Vol. 2 No.1, October.

2. Websites

1. http://www.ableindia.org
2. http://www.ableindia.org/html/india/agribiotech_biospectrum_aug04_index.html
3. http://www.ableindia.org/html/india/bioenabelers_index.html
4. http://www.ableindia.org/html/india/cluster_index.html
5. http://www.ableindia.org/html/india/biopharma_biospectrum_aug04_index.html
6. www.aponline.com
7. www.ap.gov.in
8. www.biotech-india.com
9. www.biotech.ca
10. www.biospectrum.com
11. IBID data base
12. http://www.karnataka.com/industry/biotech/
13. http://www.indianembassy.org
14. http://www.indiaserver.com
15. www.spbiotechpark.com
16. www.tsjmedia.com

Index